75p

CRICKET THROUGH THE COVERS

The author at home with his wife, Jacqueline, and
daughter, Rebecca.

CRICKET THROUGH THE COVERS

by

TOM GRAVENEY

FREDERICK MULLER LTD

LONDON

FIRST PUBLISHED BY FREDERICK MULLER LTD
IN 1958
MADE AND PRINTED IN GREAT BRITAIN BY
TAYLOR GARNETT EVANS & CO. LTD
WATFORD, HERTFORDSHIRE

CONTENTS

ILLUSTRATIONS

7

CHAPTER ONE

MY SPORTING CHILDHOOD

THE year was 1927. The Charleston was past its peak, Mussolini was pointing the way in Italy, England was slowly recovering from the general strike of the previous year.

Henri Cochet won the men's singles at Wimbledon, and at Wembley, Cardiff took the F.A. Cup when the Arsenal goalkeeper dropped the ball over his own line.

The cricket season started with a month of bright weather and a myriad runs from the bat of Wally Hammond, who shocked Gloucestershire and the cricketers-aren't-what-they-were school of diehards by equalling W. G. Grace's feat of scoring a thousand runs in May.

This was one of the feats that earned Hammond a place among Wisden's five cricketers of the year (among the others was D. R. Jardine who was to make an even greater impact on the game some five years later).

Of Hammond, Wisden said: "He is . . . a firm believer in making the bat hit the ball." Which seemed an adequate description, if nothing more.

Near the end of June, Gloucestershire beat Northamptonshire and so won their first game of the season. A seam bowler named Goddard was given an extended trial but achieved only moderate success.

Some time about the middle of June the summer dissolved in a blanket of rain that stayed static over these islands until autumn was on its way, so that in the end five county championship matches were never started and in twenty-eight others less than six hours play was possible.

On 16th June, at just about the time the monsoon hit this year of confusion, I was born at the village of Riding Mill in Northumberland. Even had I been capable of understanding the events of the time, the deeds of Hammond and Grace would have had no significance for me. The West country and Gloucestershire had no place at that time in the foreseeable future of our family.

The 16th June was a Thursday, which was just as well for it meant that the arrival of a second son had less effect on the cricketing life of my father than it would have done had it fallen on a Saturday.

The word keen is an inadequate one with which to describe my father as a sportsman. Neither is the word fanatical the right one, for that implies a ruthlessness that has never been a hallmark of our family.

When not with the family or at his work as manager of a department of Vickers Armstrong at Newcastle, he devoted himself to sport. He played cricket, golf, football and just about every ball game ever devised.

As soon as I was five, he took my elder brother Ken and myself to play golf at Ryton. Between us we had an iron, mashie, niblick and putter, and the irons he had specially made for us. Ken's children use the clubs in the garden to this day.

As golf was really the first organised game that I played, it is no real surprise that it should play such a large part in my life. And at the time when I was bouncing in and out of the England Test team, it became a matter of controversy, too. Actually, even at five, cricket was not far behind it in my affections. After experiencing my first sample of the wandering instinct that haunted the family and we had moved to Newcastle, I received my first bat.

My father presented it for courage in the face of the dentist, who removed thirteen baby teeth at one sitting. The bat was autographed, too—by Don Bradman who, at that time, as the year was 1932, was dancing around the Australian Test grounds trying to get his own bat to deliveries from Larwood, Voce and Co. which flew around his ears.

Although twenty years were to pass before I entered Test cricket, I feel sure that faint echoes of that tempestuous body-line tour still sounded about the cricket world. I believe that Nottingham, in 1948, openly murmured the word when Len Hutton was facing Keith Miller. Moreover, the hectic time Hutton underwent at the hands of Miller and Lindwall obviously strengthened his own belief in pace as the main weapon when he became captain of England.

Not that there was ever any suggestion that Hutton attempted a body-line attack, but somewhere I suspect there was a thin thread linking those searching days of 1932–33 with the emergence of Tyson and Statham.

Anyhow, at five I bade farewell to Riding Mill and had little real contact with its people again until last summer when, after a successful Test run a B.B.C. listener claimed that I had learned all my cricket in Northumberland. This claim was something of an exaggeration, but one for which I could not blame the writer. Obviously the thought that Northumberland was the county responsible for the failures I had been notching up, had got him down. This was his county's chance to recoup some of its lost prestige.

When I was six my father died.

A year later our home had been established in Fleetwood and for three years I was at the Arnold House boarding school where, unknowingly, I collected a Lancashire qualification.

Not that I did much at cricket to excite the county authorities, or even my immediate sports master. I had a liking for all games and showed no more aptitude for cricket than any other.

Not until my step-father moved to Bristol and the family followed, did I really begin to get down to cricket. And then I had the greatest stroke of luck—I came under the direction of a first-rate coach at the local Grammar school.

Like most good coaches, Mr. M. A. Tulloch was not a first-class player himself. He was a club cricketer with a good basic knowledge of the techniques of the game, yet he had the rare gift of bringing out in my brother Ken and myself whatever natural cricket ability we possessed.

Wrong coaching can be disastrous. A fault allowed to develop in a boy's technique can take years to eradicate. And the failures that pile up before that happens may be enough to kill his interest in the game.

A boy ought to be coached in such a way that he never forgets cricket is a game to be enjoyed and that the ball is there to be hit in much the same way as Hammond hit it in 1927, to the delight of Wisden. Nothing is more heartbreaking to a youngster than to tell him 'too much right hand' or 'get your foot further out' just after he has hit the ball harder than any schoolboy has ever done.

The most important item in a boy's make-up when he is playing cricket, is his zest for the game. To nag at him on technical points is to sow the seeds of disillusionment.

Thus a man who can allow a boy to enjoy his cricket and at the same time direct his game along the right lines is a good coach. And Mr. Tulloch was such a man.

Under his kindly, imaginative guidance our cricketing prowess developed in all directions. Ken established himself as a school batting star with a liking for adventurous runs. I rated myself as a bowler at a pace which I now recognise as medium, but which I then regarded as quick.

Maurice, my younger brother, was a left-arm spinner and a promising one, but his cricket hopes were shattered when he broke both legs playing Rugby. From then on his action and follow-through were affected.

In all our time at the school, Ken and I only once played together and that was when he captained The Rest against the Staff and Prefects. We won comfortably, though without much help from me.

I generally batted at number four in the school side, but nobody went on record at the time as saying: "This boy is a future England player." Neither did the thought enter my head for I would just as readily play soccer, Rugby or any other game.

Ironically, the only game that did not play a large factor in my life was golf. I did not play it again until I was sixteen, a year before I left school.

When I did start I was soon forced to give it up again for medical reasons. Ken and I used to play a game of chipping the ball to each other while it was on the move. One day Ken unleashed a tremendous drive, and I ended in hospital having stitches inserted in an eye.

My main claim to fame as a schoolboy cricketer was when I took nine wickets for 5 runs against Weston county school. This devastating bowling was strictly of the straight up and down variety, the sort, in fact, which nowadays, as a batsman, I would rather fancy!

When I was between fourteen and fifteen I used to haunt the Bristol University ground where Jack Bessant, the old Gloucestershire player, was groundsman. He knew my appetite for sport of any description and whenever a visiting team arrived short of a player he would push me forward to make up the numbers. In that way I think I played for just about every club in Bristol!

Once while away from school because of a cold I wandered along to watch a football match at the ground. I forgot all about my cold when the visitors arrived one short and I turned out at outside left for King's College, London, against Bristol Police. Some of the delight left me, however, when I returned home and my mother found out what her sick son had been doing!

But the schooldays were running out and more serious things were being mooted. Ken left and went into the Royal Marine Commandos where he became a lieutenant.

At seventeen and a half I was faced with the problem of choosing a profession. I toyed with the idea of golf and accountancy, but it looked as if adding machines and account books were going to dominate my future.

So I went on a tour of several accountants' offices in Bristol and was appalled. Never had I seen such dingy, miserable places, but what was I to do? I had to take up work of some kind.

I deferred the question by joining the army.

Once in khaki I added to my list of sports activities by

entering the unit boxing tournaments. I became one of the few people in the history of that bruising sport who could box with a reasonable expectation of not being hurt. This was a comforting thought that sprang not from any great prowess with my fists, but because I had suddenly shot up to six feet.

As my weight was only nine stone two pounds, this meant that I operated among the lightweights, and by propping my opponents on the end of a spidery left-hand I found that few of them could reach me. Boxing without pain seemed a reasonable sport to me at the time.

In the spring of 1946 I was commissioned with the Gloucestershire Regiment, and with its uncanny sense of the occasion, the War Office managed to post me abroad on my birthday.

My destination was Egypt where I was put into a transit camp and spent the first five days doing nothing. Of the following sixteen days fourteen were devoted to playing cricket.

After that I was posted to Athens with the Hampshire Regiment. More cricket, only this time played on matting over concrete. Eventually when the Brigade broke up, I and five others were posted to the Royal Artillery.

Six months later I was asked if I wished to transfer to that regiment permanently. I said "no" and was promptly ordered to an anti-terrorist camp in Kenya.

On the way south I stopped off at the transit camp where I had played my first cricket outside England. I never got any farther because the Commanding Officer recognised me and said: "You're the fellow who plays a bit of cricket. Would you like to be our sports officer?" Thus I reached the peak of my military career.

Meanwhile, Ken had been demobilised but was not taking kindly to civilian life. He was restless and was talking of going back into the Army.

Once again I began to consider the question of my own future and came to the conclusion that I would stay in the Army as a regular soldier. It seemed a life to which my talents, or lack of them, were admirably suited.

Before making up his mind about rejoining the Services, Ken, who had been playing cricket for Stoke Bishop, thought he would have one final effort at establishing a civilian career. He obtained a trial with Gloucestershire and created such a favourable impression that he was engaged by the county club.

In August 1947 I came home on leave. Gloucestershire were second in the county championship and enjoying, with the rest of cricket, a golden summer. That was the year in which Denis Compton and Bill Edrich shattered batting records with the gusto of men having the spree of a life-time.

One or two of the regular Gloucestershire players were beginning to feel the strain and as they stood down from some Sunday charity matches I stepped in on the introduction of Ken, who said: "This is my brother. I can't get the ball past his bat."

Without threatening to live up to this build-up, I scored a few runs and was then approached by the county secretary, Colonel Henson, who invited me to join the Gloucestershire staff when I left the army.

This was quite an extraordinary position to be in for although I had contemplated the idea of taking up golf professionally, cricket as a career had never entered my head.

But I had little hesitation in accepting the offer, even though I rated my chances of making the grade as a county player rather low. After three months playing, I thought my pessimism was well-founded.

CHAPTER TWO

AN UNHAPPY DÉBUT

THOSE first three months in 1948 almost ended my career before it had properly started. Every misfortune that could strike a cricketer struck me, so that in no time I felt there was no place in the Professional game for me.

On 1st May, I strolled on to the beautiful Parks ground at Oxford with the rest of the Gloucestershire side, a newcomer entering the exciting world of big cricket hoping, just like every man before me and since, that I would not fail.

Oxford University batted past the three hundred mark, and then came our turn to bat. Graveney T. W. was on the card to open with George Emmett. I was in the position that has caused controversy throughout my career with the man who, when the fancy takes him, is the greatest stroke player in English cricket. Emmett, on his day, can annihilate any class of bowling.

And that was one of his days. He carried his bat for an unbeaten century, even though the University, with Kardar doing most of the damage, put us out for 156.

I was one of the few men Kardar did not trouble. I departed long before he came to the bowling crease—caught Travers bowled Whitcombe 0.

Overall, my memories of this game are not cheerful. In the University innings I was fielding on the boundary to Tom Goddard when Donald Carr swung lustily and the catch came straight to me. Into my hands went the ball—and out again.

The weather was cold. But not half as cold as the hand that clutched at my heart.

The county were ready enough to forgive, if not to forget, and I was kept in the side to take my runs off Worcestershire —four in each innings. I was given a good trial without showing much sign of taking advantage of it.

I was elated to reach double figures against Sussex before Alan Oakman dismissed me, and then came 26 against Lancashire.

The first milestone—I almost called it millstone—in my career arrived in the next match. In mid-July against Derbyshire at Bristol I collected a 'pair'. Off the third ball I received in the first innings I was caught by Pope in Gladwin's leg-trap. On the second day we were left with about twenty minutes batting. As I walked off the field, my morale by this time in tatters, I heard the words that to this day make my spine prickle and my ears drum.

Skipper B. O. Allen turned to me and said: "Put on your pads. It's your chance to get off the mark."

It was an opportunity for which I was far from grateful. With Colin Scott, the medium pace bowler, I went out to withstand all the ferocity and guile of Cliff Gladwin and Les Jackson looking for a quick wicket before the close. They got it. Mine.

I suppose I had reached the stage in this disastrous opening to my career when I constantly feared the worst and so made myself a more ready victim.

Be that as it may, I tipped the first delivery from Jackson to George Dawkes and so did my bit towards helping Derbyshire become the first side to win at Bristol since the war. After that I was dropped.

Since I had started playing first class cricket I had not touched a golf club. When I learned that my presence was no longer required in the first team, a flame of defiance lit up my misery and I gathered my clubs and went to Henbury where I had two games. After that I felt better. Golf, I reckoned, was a great game.

Two memories come back to me from this period of failure. One was of a couple of Derbyshire players suspiciously eyeing a full-length portrait of W. G. Grace at the wicket with his upright stance, beard a-bristle and left toe cocked in the air.

After a long, silent, critical inspection, one asked: "Why's he got his toe up in the air like that?"

More contemplation.

"To trap the yorker," said the other. They went away satisfied.

The other memory arises from the match with Yorkshire at Bristol in May. Brian Sellers made his first appearance on the ground after voicing strong criticism of Wally Hammond's captaincy of the M.C.C. side on the 1946–47 tour of Australia.

Sellers has always been one to speak his mind, and he did it on the subject of Hammond with great clarity and pointedness. Yet there were those in Gloucestershire and other parts of the world who were prepared to believe that the fault lay not so much with Hammond but in the decision to send a team overseas when English cricket was still weak from the war and the Australian side so powerful.

Be that as it may, Sellers appeared at Bristol and was duly barracked. As he walked to the wicket there were shouts of "Fetch Wally."

"That's reet," he called back. "I'm here. T'other bloke isn't."

Sellers had reason to remember that trip into the West country. He fell victim to the greatest session of aggressive stroke play it has ever been my pleasure to see.

The Yorkshire captain set us to score 389 in four and a half hours. Charlie Barnett and George Emmett crashed off with an opening stand of 226 in two hours and the match was as good as won.

If ever two men were created for a situation it was this pair. Emmett, dapper, neat but strong, was the perfect foil to Barnett, a man who played shots from positions which no other orthodox player could have hit them. We won by six wickets with forty-three minutes to spare.

18

When it was all over, Sellers appeared in the doorway of our dressing-room.

"Well played, you lot," he said. "But I'll ne'er declare against yer again."

Looking back, I think it was the decision to drop me which nearly finished my career. If Jack Crapp and George Emmett had not been called up for Test service against Australia, I do not think I would have played again that season. And, in that event, the county might easily have decided not to re-engage me.

As it was, Emmett and Crapp were required by England and the Gloucestershire selection committee, with only thirteen professionals on the staff, had no option but to pick me. And fortunately for me, the nightmare ended.

Batting against Hampshire at Bournemouth on a turning wicket, I missed a half century by three runs. Against Somerset at Bristol I was 81 not out. In a month I made 600 runs—it still ranks as one of my best scoring sequences—and my first hundred in county cricket came off the Combined Services' bowlers at Gloucester after I had made 89 in the first innings.

Thus was success born out of failure. Needless to say, nobody was more pleased at the turn of events than I.

Barnett's kindly understanding had much to do with this sudden flood of runs. He came to me in the misery of my early days and encouraged me not to despair. On one occasion I confided to him that I just could not get the ball away. It would not seem to travel off the bat.

He took my bat, tried it, commented that he did not wonder that I never hit the ball with that thing, and presented me with his own bat, the one he used in the Tests against Australia.

It was a glorious piece of wood, probably the most beautifully alive bat I ever possessed. I used it from what I might term the start of my comeback, right through to the end of the season. I owe Barnett a great deal for his helping hand when my cricketing future was in the balance. He was one of the most unselfish sportsmen I have ever met.

Perhaps fortunately, looking at events in retrospect, I was not selected for the match against the Australians at Bristol when Gloucestershire were put to the sword with an ease and ruthlessness that was almost embarrassing. The tourists scored 774 for seven declared, which was their highest score of a summer in which they ran riot. It was the highest score by an Australian team against an English county and ironically, was compiled without the help of cricket's greatest run machine, Don Bradman, who stood down from the match. His presence was not missed, although it meant that I never saw him strike the ball.

Although not picked for the match I had a good view of it because I spent most of the time on the field as a substitute fielder.

The left-handed Arthur Morris assumed the rôle of executioner-in-chief, hitting a century before lunch, and another between lunch and tea. Altogether he scored 290, a breath-taking display that was produced purely for the benefit of Tom Goddard.

Goddard, his hands the size of cushions, could be devastating with his off-breaks, especially on a wearing pitch. He was a man Australia had no wish to meet in a Test match if conditions should help him, so after he won the toss Lindsay Hassett went to Morris as he was strapping on his pads, and told him: "If this fellow Goddard comes on give him stick. We don't want him in the Tests."

The plan was similar to that by which Hammond temporarily dismissed Fleetwood-Smith from the Australian Test selectors' reckoning before the war.

Morris, ever a cheerful cricketer, showed such relish for his job that long before the innings was over Goddard had retired to the dressing-room with an injured finger.

The Gloucestershire off-spinner, backed by the experience of decades of first class cricket was just incapable of containing the exuberant Morris. As the ball sailed from Goddard's hand so Morris danced down the wicket to hunt it out, and whenever the bowler dropped it short, he lay back and hit it harder.

The memory of that day will haunt Goddard.

Sam Loxton scored a century and Neil Harvey missed one by five runs. In fact by the end of the innings runs had ceased to mean anything.

My own view of most of the batting was obtained from the covers. We were overcrowded in that region, but we still could not stop the ball. Frankly, I was amazed that Goddard, the man I had so often seen tame batsmen, could be hit so hard.

Such was my lack of confidence at that time after my string of failures that I did not relish the ball coming my way in case it brought yet another indignity in its wake.

You must remember that I was the youngest member of the side, feeling a not-very-successful way into the game among players whose reputations were thoroughly established.

Whatever help they gave me, I always felt acutely conscious of my unique position in the side. In short, I was lonely.

Nothing can be worse in the approach of a young cricketer than this feeling of not wanting to be busily engaged on the field. Indeed, not until he wants the ball to come to him, tries to will it in his direction, can the aspiring youngster hope to blossom into a player of adequate merit.

That is the strength of most of the young players who are reaching for greatness today. They just cannot have enough of the ball. I hope that I, too, have now learned the lesson of those formative years as a county cricketer.

The crowning blow for Tom Goddard came when he batted in the game against the Australians. After all the suffering that had been inflicted upon him as a bowler, he was offered a slow full toss down the leg side by Ian Johnson so that he could get off the mark.

Being a gentleman, he refrained from hitting it for four. Instead he tried to push it away for a single. He succeeded only in getting a top edge to it and the ball dropped gently into the wicket keeper's hands.

Nought on top of nought for 186! Such a fate!

Gloucestershire's only consolation from the match came

in the shape of a century by Jack Crapp, scored off the not inconsiderable attack of Ray Lindwall, Sam Loxton, Ian Johnson, Doug Ring and Colin McCool, strengthened by the puzzling slows of those 'ace spinners' Arthur Morris and Lindsay Hassett.

This was my first look at Lindwall with his smooth, accelerating run and his slingy low-armed action. I did not bat against him until 1953 and it was interesting to note the change that had come into his bowling during that time.

In 1948 he was the only bowler I saw to lift the ball above stump height on that torpid Bristol strip of turf. For years the pitches in Gloucestershire provided little encouragement to the fast bowlers, which is probably the reason why George Lambert toiled so long without real support. As for the Bristol pitch it possessed the liveliness of cotton-wool where pace bowlers were concerned, although since the war it has generally aided the spin bowlers (despite Goddard's experience against the Australians). In 1947 it was even treated with sand.

The Lindwall of 1948 bowled only away swingers and his celebrated yorker, quite the most coldly, destructive ball delivered by any fast bowler during my time.

By 1953 Lindwall had served a spell in Lancashire League cricket and added the in-swinger to his range, even though there were experts who claimed that this type of delivery was impossible with his low action. There was much eating of words when Lindwall not only bowled the in-swinger, but bowled it with all the mastery and accuracy which hall-marked his bowling.

But while variety had been added to the Lindwall attack in 1953, his overall pace dropped a little. He was still genuinely fast and when he wanted he could let slip a delivery that was as quick as anything he ever bowled.

Little point is served in trying to guess whether he was easier to play in 1948 than he was in 1953. I can only say that Lindwall was a most troublesome customer at any time in any conditions.

The Australian visit to Bristol gave me my first taste of

the most arduous job in cricket. That of being twelfth man in a match against the touring side.

Never have I seen so many bats, books and scorecards piled high for me to take into their dressing-room for signature. And it was my responsibility to see that each item got back to its owner—a nightmare job when dealing with a light-hearted touring side which, without being deliberately callous, was not as attentive to these details as the autograph hunters would have wished.

I found too, that for the three days, I gathered about me a circle of friends far wider than my doubtful reputation as a budding cricketer deserved. They all called me Tom, mostly wanted to meet the Australians, and were often inquiring about obtaining Test match tickets.

By the end of the third day I was limp. I do not think I have ever worked so hard in any sphere of cricket and I was flabbergasted later when George Emmett laughed at my experiences and promptly began to tell me of his sufferings at Leeds.

Emmett was twelfth man for England in the fourth Test at Leeds. What with taking drinks out on to the field during play, carrying lunches to the dressing-room for anyone who wanted it there, looking after autographs, ordering taxis, running the bath, he reckoned it was seven o'clock before he had finished his chores on the last day. That job nearly broke Emmett's heart.

Fortunately the twelfth man job during a Test match is not so onerous now. Many of the duties are taken over by the masseur and dressing-room attendant.

At the end of the season I appeared in the Hastings Festival. Since that year I have been invited to the Scarborough Festival, and with all credit to the other festivals, to the work that the organisers, put in on them and to their determination to give both players and public an enjoyable time, I must say that there is no Festival to equal that of the Yorkshire seaside resort.

For players possibly jaded by a surfeit of cricket and

responsibility, it is the ideal way to close the season. The cricket is good, the social spirit marvellous, and Scarborough invariably provides enough enjoyable memories to keep a cricketer warm throughout a long, dark winter.

The Festival match at Hastings was born out of the usual air of fantasy that stamps matches in any festival.

I appeared in the North v. South game, inexplicably on the side of the North, together with my county colleagues Barnett and Emmett. Somehow Sam Cook, our Gloucestershire slow left-arm bowler, qualified for the South.

When he came in to bat there occurred an incident similar to that between Tom Goddard and the Australians. With Barnett bowling and the occasion light-hearted, there seemed no doubt that Sam would be allowed off the mark.

First ball, Barnett let go an in-swinger, Cook stabbed at it and Emmett at leg-slip dived wide to take a brilliant catch. Poor Sam just stood stock-still in shocked amazement, then slowly looked at the grinning faces of we Gloucestershire 'exiles' and departed.

In the pavilion afterwards he observed philosophically: "You Northerners play it hard."

So, after a grim beginning, my first season passed fairly successfully. My main weakness was my play off the backfoot. It was good enough for club cricket, but far too vulnerable against top-class bowlers moving the ball, both through the air and off the pitch.

With the help of others, I analysed that much of the fault lay in my abnormally high backlift which was accentuated by using a long handle bat. In an effort to curb it, I tried using a short handle bat in the nets and since that day have used nothing else, even though I am over six feet tall.

During the winter I took up a post as coach at the county's indoor cricket school at Bristol. Teaching the youngsters how to place their feet when playing a shot, helped to eradicate my own errors. So often it was like looking at a moving picture of myself playing a stroke and instinctively I knew where I was going wrong.

When I batted at the school, I was under the critical eye of Charlie Parker, another of the great coaches with which my career has been blessed.

He harangued me from sun-up to sundown in his efforts to tighten my technique. The half volley I would hammer with ease, but as soon as the length of the ball made it impossible for me to play strokes off the front foot I was struggling.

Parker would shout at me down the net: "You'll never be any good until you learn to play back."

Then I would make a superhuman effort and in, perhaps twenty-five minutes batting, would succeed in going back twice.

That was the signal for Charlie to explode again. "If I bowled to you," he roared, "you would never get a half volley. Bowlers have got brains as well."

Ironically, in view of my own early fears, my off-driving was already being compared with that of Hammond, a comparison that well meaning but not always wise people have made throughout my cricketing life.

Hammond's deeds will be remembered as long as old men in Panama hats dream cricket and little boys play it in back alleys with an old tin can. Hammond is one of the immortals, and to link my name with his is just too silly for words.

And for those who claim that on the evidence of their own eyes they know that I copied my off-side play from that of Hammond, sadly I would point out that Hammond retired before I was even thought of by the county.

In short, the only thing Wally Hammond and I have in common is that we both played for Gloucestershire.

CHAPTER THREE

THE WEST INDIES MARCH OF TRIUMPH

WHAT a beautiful, heart-warming season 1949 was after all that had gone before. To start with, I began the summer as a capped county player, my batting technique had improved considerably and I began to think—hopefully let it be admitted —in terms of a place in England's team.

Back to Oxford I went for Gloucestershire's traditional opening match of the season, the memory of that nought in my first innings in county cricket tucked furtively in the corner of my mind.

In the first innings of this match I fared only little better— just three runs to be precise. The second innings put the start of the season into perspective, *my* kind of perspective.

I scored a hundred in two hours and Gloucestershire limped to an exciting draw with the last wicket pair, George Lambert and Sam Cook, holding out for fifteen minutes.

Runs kept coming steadily in the opening matches with another hundred in the fourth game of the season against Nottinghamshire at Trent Bridge.

Not until the fifth match did we play on a home ground.

In mid-June we met the Combined Services at Bristol, and although I was not in the side it was the first look I took at a player who I am sure will rank among the greatest the game has ever known.

He appeared on the card as Writer P. B. H. May, and he scored 80 in the first innings (bowled by my brother Ken) and 90 not out in the second. As a young batsman trying to find my own way in the game, I was immensely impressed at the composure of May at the crease.

At that time he had played all his first-class cricket at the Universities and in the Services side, yet he showed the bearing of a man who has grown wise and hard in the saving of lost causes. By that I do not mean that he was not an attractive player—he was, is and always will be. May is one of those stroke players who, when he is in form, paints this game of cricket in the most beautiful colours.

But even as a youth he always gave the impression that the bowler had not been born who could gain a moral ascendancy over him. Indeed, he would look the master right up to the ball which dismissed him.

Thus must the youthful Bradman and Hammond have looked as they were making their young ways.

My own batting successes went on. I took 96 off Middlesex for whom the then-fiery Bill Edrich and Laurie Gray, now an umpire, shared the opening attack. I was going for what would have been my eleventh boundary to complete a century when I was caught at deep mid-on.

By the end of the season I had mustered fifteen hundred runs and my technique was as sound as it ever will be. Throughout this summer and the following one, I could play either forward or back with equal facility.

By 1951 my batting had hit another unexpected patch of trouble. I, who dreamed at nights of whipping away succulent half volleys on the off-stump, suddenly found that the power had gone from my off-side play.

I would strike the ball wide of cover point and then watch unbelievingly as the fielder moved easily across and stopped it without any effort. Eventually I reached the stage when I found it impossible to play forward, although my ability to place the ball wide of mid-on had improved out of all recognition.

My career has been spattered with these sudden shifting of stresses in my batting. At one time I was known as a player with no strokes on the leg-side. Yet only a couple of years ago

I was nicknamed the 'On-side King' for shots that I played to leg from outside the off-stump on the true West Indian pitches.

But back to 1949, the year I played against my first touring side—the New Zealanders. They won comfortably enough at Bristol with some excellent batting from Wally Hadlee and Martin Donnelly.

Each time my innings was ended by that tantalising left-hander Tom Burtt, a slow spinner of immaculate length who tied down England's best batsmen in the Tests.

Burtt, who bowled almost entirely in a defensive capacity, had a natural dislike for being hit. The more a batsman went after him, the wider he bowled—and always with the most perfect control—to a packed off-side field.

To play Burtt successfully in those days was almost always a test of patience because sooner or later if a batsman kept chivvying him he would be caught at cover failing to reach the pitch of the ball, or else was stumped.

I learned the lesson effectively in this match, my second innings ending stumped Mooney bowled Burtt 1.

The consistency of Burtt did probably more than anything to bring to an end the practice of playing three-day Test matches. He proved beyond a shadow of doubt that in modern cricket, with its highly developed field-placing and bowling techniques, a game could be closed down on a good wicket.

Such a position was neither in the interest of the game nor the crowds. Cricket is essentially an entertainment and as such the spectators have a reasonable right to expect a result to their matches, all other things being equal. In 1949 that was not the case and so the five-day Test match was ushered in for general use, with the result that now we have gone to the other extreme whereby countries whose standard of play is not really worthy of five-day Tests, are automatically granted them.

Such is the importance of prestige attached to international sport these days that any other line of action is hardly possible.

If three-day Tests were ever to succeed there would need

to be a complete change in the approach of the world's cricketers towards the game.

For a game to produce a definite decision in three days it is necessary not only for the batsmen to attack the bowlers, but for the bowlers to attack the batsmen.

When scoring is slow, it is easy for watchers to blame the batsman. But no batsman worthy of his reputation and jealous of his Test place is going to throw his wicket away chasing bowlers with a deep-rooted objection to bowling at the stumps.

It stands to reason that if bowlers attack the stumps they will get more wickets. They will also concede more runs.

The formula is as simple as that, yet in the involved and heartbreaking tactics that go towards making Test matches, there seems little room for the enactment of these basic principles of the game.

Everybody is to blame and nobody is to blame. The heavy yoke of pride and prestige is around the captain's neck and so Test matches are played harder than any other form of cricket. And that is precisely the way the public wants it to be, so that all in all we get just the kind of cricket we deserve.

The ironic thing about this run of drawn matches with the New Zealanders was that it influenced the Board of Control for Test matches at Home to recommend that five days be allotted to each of the four Tests with the West Indies in 1950.

And what a holocaust that decision brought in its wake!

As the sleight of hand practised by Sonny Ramadhin and Alf Valentine bewildered our batsmen, so I began to believe more strongly that there might be a place in the England side for me.

The skill of these remarkable bowlers was to harass the English batting for years, yet their first trip to England was something in the nature of a gamble. Both were young, unknown quantities in the field of top-class cricket, yet they turned out to be one of the greatest spinning combinations in the history of Test cricket.

From 1950 onwards they were the West Indies' Test attack, and for all the batting brilliance of Weekes, Worrell and

Walcott, it was they more than anybody else who sent England plunging to 3-1 defeat in the series.

With men of the calibre of the three Ws backed by Stollmeyer and Rae, the batting possessed both depth and quality. Yet in the bowling line Ramadhin and Valentine took fifty-nine of the side's seventy-seven Test wickets.

The West Indians were aided in their march of triumph by the fact that England were in an interim period of reconstruction which hits all sides. Immediately behind us was the unconvincing, drawn series against New Zealand, a country with a limited population from which to choose her cricketers, and only a little way further back was the memory of that fearful drubbing the Australians had handed us in 1948.

In vivid contrast, although we did not know it at the time (and nobody in 1950 would have believed it anyway, as they surveyed the smoking ruins of English cricket), there lay only two years ahead the start of a spell of success that was going to put us on top of the cricket world.

Another factor of importance in this England tale of woe was the run of injuries sustained by our Test players. Len Hutton missed one Test with an injured finger, Denis Compton was out for most of the season with a knee injury that was to grow in dark significance as the seasons rolled by, and Bill Edrich was unable to play in two of the Tests.

So the university men, the players professionals refer to light-heartedly and with no attempt at malice, as the 'College Lads', were given their fling in international cricket.

John Dewes, David Sheppard, Doug Insole and Hubert Doggart all played without showing much sign that they were going to stem the flow of calypsos that poured forth from the crowds of excited West Indian supporters who packed our grounds—steel bands as well. May, quite the best of the bunch even then, was the only University player of note not to get an England place that season.

That the university contingent generally failed is not surprising. They were suddenly exposed to the full blast of public attention and Test atmosphere at a time when a pair of bowlers were gathering an aura of mystery around them as they wrecked the country's best professional batting. Old hands who had been earning their living at the game for fifteen years could not tell which way Ramadhin was going to turn the ball, so how could young men hope to whose cricket was nurtured on the placid Fenner's strip?

Unfortunately, these young men were cast into the furnace on the strength of Cambridge University's performance in holding the West Indians to a draw in mid-May.

In that match 1,324 runs were scored for the loss of only seven wickets. West Indians, who spend their lives playing on plumb pitches, had never seen anything like this one. Apparently it not only went out of its way to help the batsman, but it came precious close to insulting the bowler.

In that welter of runs Sheppard and Dewes put on 343 in under five hours for the first wicket and so established a world record for an opening stand against the West Indians.

Doggart, at number three, scored 71, and just to get the true nature of this pitch from purely statistical sources, I would point out that for the West Indies Christiani scored 111, Worrell 160 and Weekes 304 not out.

Before the Test series was over all three of the Cambridge men had played for England. Dewes appeared in two matches (four innings) for a total of 87 runs, 67 of which came in one innings; Doggart, with the same number of chances made 11 less runs; and Sheppard was the comparative success of the trio hitting 11 and 29 at the Oval in his only appearance.

This analysis of the 1950 performances of these three players is not produced in an effort to belittle them—their performance on later occasions proved their worth—but it does help support a theory of mine.

And it is that extreme care should be taken in assessing university cricketers. It is one of the hardest jobs in the world.

Both teams play on wickets at the Parks and Fenner's that are a batsman's dream of paradise. One need have no pretences to greatness to make centuries on these pitches.

Neither, unless it is at the start of the season, do the

counties field their best teams when they play the Universities. Usually the stars take a rest and youngsters are introduced into the side.

In these circumstances when they are often playing what is little better than glorified club cricket, I do not think it right that a university man should be considered for a Test place. This sudden emergence into the hard light of the Test arena places too great an onus both on them and on their more experienced England colleagues.

Far better that the university players should be judged on what they do *away* from the Parks and Fenner's. I know their short tours generally occur too late in the summer to have much influence on selection for current Test matches, but at least they supply a yardstick on which future consideration can be based.

There also appeared in the disastrous 1950 series a player who, I feel, has been robbed of his rightful Test place by circumstances.

Doug Insole appeared in the Third Test at Nottingham and scored 21 in his two innings. In his first he was l.b.w. bowled Ramadhin for 21; in his second, stumped Walcott bowled Ramadhin 0.

In those figures are written the fate of Insole, one of the hardest fighting batsmen of my time. Perhaps Doug does not bring much beauty to the art of batting. Maybe he does offend every canon of the game with his cross-batted shovel shot that puts the ball round to the leg-side.

No, he is not a charmer, but he is a fighter, and I know which all the Test captains I have served under would rather have in their side.

To the pace bowler with the new ball that describes violent arcs in the summer air, or to the slow bowler who makes the ball turn and caper off a helpful pitch, Insole, with that atrocious cross-bat, looks an easy victim. But that he never is.

He can make runs when every fate decrees he and the side are lost. In and out of the England team he bounced, ever

(*Above*) Peter May and Colin Cowdrey applauded by West Indies after their match-saving partnership, First Test, Edgbaston, 1957.

(*Below*) Denis Compton plays his favourite sweep stroke.

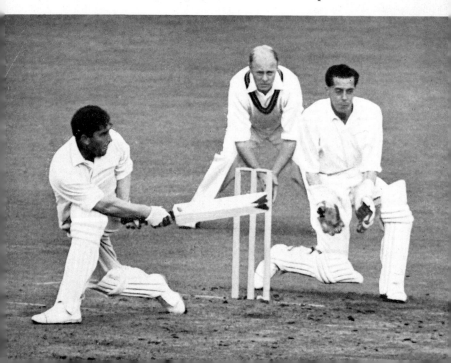

(*Left*) No, it's not Carmen Miranda but England's wicket-keeper, Godfrey Evans, in a fancy dress competition on board ship.

(*Below*) Peter Richardson (right) as Liberace, Frank Tyson as George and Harold Dalton, M.C.C.'s masseur, as 'Mom'.

cheerful and enthusiastic, fighting down the prejudice his style naturally breeds, until it seemed that last winter in South Africa he had established himself. I was not on that tour but his figures speak for themselves, and players who were there tell me that his cricket was hall-marked with courage.

It is my sincere belief that on the evidence of his South African performances, Doug Insole should have a permanent place in the England side.

But waiting round the corner for him was Ramadhin. And Ramadhin is the man who has put the doubt back into Insole's future.

Insole, for all his sharp eye and reflexes, can make nothing of the little West Indian. He can read his spin no better now probably than he did in 1950, and that unfortunate fact was proved as early as the First Test match of last year when Ramadhin captured his wicket each innings, the second time for a 'duck' when England were in as bad a position as a side has ever been.

This mastery of the West Indian over Insole probably helped in my rehabilitation as a Test cricketer, but that does not stop it being a tragedy for both England and the Essex player.

While discussing the West Indians' efforts of 1950, I think the time appropriate to pay tribute to Sonny Ramadhin, then at the peak of his prowess. In 1957 the massive English batting chipped some of the polish off his reputation, so it is as well to be reminded just how great he was.

When Ramadhin played in England in 1950, he was twenty years of age and unknown. By the end of the season he had taken one hundred and thirty-five wickets, more than any other West Indian bowler had ever taken in this country, and established a mastery over English batsmen that was almost magical. His bowling possessed all the virtues of a good performer—length, direction, variation—combined with this fantastic ability to spin the ball either way with a hand action that was almost unreadable.

Yet this tiny man with the ability to shatter reputations,

came from no real cricket background. His father, apparently, knew nothing about the game—no more than his mother!

The young Ramadhin first played the game at a missionary school in Trinidad and, like most boys, he saw himself as a batsman. He even won a cup for the number of runs he scored, which is a source of amazement now that his batting has become something of a joke.

Not until he left school and joined the local club did he start bowling, and only then because the bigger players elbowed the tiny tot away from the batting crease in the practice nets. From those unlikely beginnings, Ramadhin, the bowler developed, until eventually he was given two matches for Trinidad and then shipped on the boat for England and the Test matches. Promptly he became a legend.

I doubt if at any time in the history of cricket there has been such a sudden and unexpected surge to fame. Normally a slow bowler's art develops with time and experience. With Ramadhin it just seems to have been latent, awaiting the chance to come to the surface.

By the time the West Indians visited Gloucestershire at Cheltenham, the Ramadhin reputation was already sky high. In the course of two days he managed to add to it as the county scuttled in and out for 69 and 97. I fell to him both times, bowled the first time and caught the second. I feel it would make interesting reading to know how many of his victims Ramadhin had bowled or l.b.w. My overall impression of his accuracy was that it was uncanny.

A good example of the skill of Ramadhin came in this match when he twice bowled Andy Wilson, our wicket-keeper, for his first 'pair' in county cricket.

Indignity was heaped upon indignity in the second innings. Determined that he would get off the mark, and cautious with it, Andy put his bat over his shoulder as the ball pitched outside the off-stump, confident that it was the leg-break. Unbelievingly he marched pavilion-wards, his leg stump groggy.

Wilson could be deceived like this, yet he was an experienced cricketer, a useful batsman, and as wicket-keeper a man well versed in the arts of watching a bowler's hand.

As Ramadhin and Valentine laid the English batting low, so a touch of realism came into my dream of one day being a Test batsman. For some time I had been referred to as a future England player and in 1950, with 1,600 runs in a wet season, I topped the Gloucestershire averages even though the usually soft pitches gave little scope for my fotward shots.

Against Sussex at Worthing in July I scored the first double century of my career in just under six hours batting. I cannot recall giving a chance, but I can remember the pitch—and that memory fills me with joy even at this distance of time.

But its character changed for Sussex after rain and in stepped Tom Goddard and his off-breaks to pick up thirteen wickets.

The season was an unpredictable one for Gloucestershire. We finished in seventh place in the championship, so that we were neither better nor worse off than the previous year. Yet we won only six games and for a side that looked so good on paper, our displays were disappointingly uneven.

Annoying as these lapses may be on occasions, they also contribute towards the aura of unpredictable charm that surrounds West country cricket. We have always played the game as well as we can without losing sight of the fact that it is essentially an enjoyment. We may lose wickets and matches attempting shots that would make Surrey and Yorkshire players blench, but we take pride that there is no ruthlessness in our cricket make-up.

And I for one think Gloucestershire cricket is all the better for being without it.

CHAPTER FOUR

PLAYING FOR ENGLAND

THE 1951 season brought me an England place, an intriguing future in the limitless field of international cricket, and a lot more worries about gaining and keeping a place.

Ambition is a funny thing in cricket. It spurred me on towards that England place, and then when I secured it I realised that I was going to have to work even harder to retain it.

I knew at once that this would be a vital season for me. The South Africans were here to play five-day Test cricket and early season runs assumed more importance than ever before. The start was not without grounds for hope.

At Oxford in the first game of the season I hit 201 and so equalled my previous season's score against Sussex—the highest up to then of my first-class career. In the next match against Somerset I collected a half century.

Then came the match which was going to put me in the Test selectors' notebooks—or otherwise. The South Africans came to Bristol with an attack that boasted the genuine, uncontrolled speed of Cuan McCarthy, the pace of Michael Melle, the off-spin of Athol Rowan, the slow left-handers of 'Tufty' Mann and the stock bowling of Percy Mansell. We already knew, or guessed enough about the South African side to know that this was pretty near a Test attack. In fact, looking back, apart from the tireless Geoff Chubb, it was just about the best attack the Springboks could produce that year.

These bowlers were either going to put me out of Test reckoning, or into it. There were no half measures about it for the First Test was only three weeks away. To save you all the tedious details of a rags-to-riches success story, let me say at once that I took the chance, scored 37 in the first innings and missed a century in the second by seven runs.

When I left the field at the end of that second knock, it was practically to jig-time. I think I even forgot to be disappointed at missing the century because I knew then that each time the England selectors met that season, the name Tom Graveney was going to be among the runners.

But it was impossible to be completely selfish about that match.

Without any of us fully realising it, it was the beginning of the end of two careers, one a great one, the other full of promise.

In the trial in the nets before the match my brother Ken broke down and could not play in the game, and during my second innings Dudley Nourse broke a thumb trying to field a cover drive from me.

I remember the moment clearly. Mansell pitched a delivery short outside the off-stump and I lay back and thrashed it into the covers. Probably because the day was raw and his hands were cold, Nourse did not get fully behind the ball which jumped and struck his thumb.

An operation was necessary on the thumb which was wired and Nourse bravely went off to the First Test to lead South Africa to their first Test win in sixteen years. His own contribution was 208 before he was run out, and during that innings his hand swelled so badly that once he left the crease he dropped out of the game altogether.

That innings must rate high among the courageous events of Test cricket, yet it took its toll. When Nourse got back to South Africa at the end of the tour, he retired from the game. I suppose it might be said that in my efforts to break into international cricket, I put Dudley Nourse out of it. Fortunately we don't know about these things at the time.

While England, whipped at Nottingham, came back to level the series at Lord's through the off-spinning of Roy Tattersall on a wet wicket, I went on steadily compiling runs in the county games. Then in July pleasure in Gloucestershire, elation in the dressing room and near-hysteria in the Graveney family circle when it became known I was to report to Manchester for the Third Test.

Words are a colourless medium through which to describe how I felt that day. I was in an England Test party, admittedly with little chance of playing, after a beginning which suggested that cricket was not going to be my profession. Probably only some wild, triumphant chord of music could adequately express my emotion at being included among the cricket powers in the land.

So off to Manchester to face the hard labour of the twelfth man job. I was there to soak up and acclimatise myself to that indefinable tension known as Test match atmosphere. And I got plenty of it in the very spot where it is most noticeable—at the crease on a wicket which must have been conceived in hell.

On the morning of the match I was preparing to parcel up autograph books and stook bats for signature in the dressing room, when Freddie Brown, the England captain, walked up and said: "Denis is unfit. You're playing. Best of luck."

Compton, who had been nursing an injured toe, decided at the last minute that he was unfit to play. So the crowd sighed that they were not to see their beloved Denis—a hero at Old Trafford ever since that great hundred against the Australians in 1948—and Graveney was in.

Out we went to field and before I had time to make up my mind whether I was scared or excited, we were plunging into a match that for sheer incident was memorable.

The fourth ball of the match Eric Rowan pushed towards Freddie Brown at leg-slip and Alec Bedser was on his way towards a match analysis of twelve for 112. The Surrey giant bowled as well in this game as I ever saw him.

On a wet pitch he intermingled swerve and lift with that magically controlled leg-cutter so that long before the match was over he had the South Africans in a state of mass hypnosis. Only Clive van Ryneveld in the first innings played him like a man who recognised that he was human.

And this Bedser triumph was enacted in wind so strong that I could not reach the wicket with a throw from long-leg.

The Springboks' struggle was great fun to watch, but they were to have an even more amusing time on the third day after the second had been washed out by rain.

I took my place on the balcony awaiting my first innings in Test cricket as Hutton and Jack Ikin went out to bat. Carefully I watched as Athol Rowan opened the bowling, and then came the delivery that made my mouth drop open and the breath catch in my throat.

The second ball from this slow off-spinner sprang off a length like a mad thing and struck Hutton on the shoulder. "This," I thought to myself, "is a fine time to make a Test debut."

Before long I was having a closer look at Rowan. That day he made the ball jump like a sorbo ball, particularly while the wicket was at its worst for ninety minutes before lunch. For forty-five of those minutes I batted as I had never batted before.

At the other end Mann turned the ball so far towards the slips that I would have needed a lacrosse stick to have reached him. When I came in after that innings—I did not bat again—I was delighted that on my first occasion in the big atmosphere I could bat well above myself. Both technique and temperament had come through the test satisfactorily in conditions in which the life of a batsman was strictly limited.

England passed the South African score through the courage of Freddie Brown, the resourcefulness as batsmen of those two bowlers Bedser and Jim Laker, and through a quite beautiful little innings from Willie Watson.

Brown had come back from skippering the M.C.C. side in Australia only a few months previously, with a huge reputation for putting guts and character into his cricket. Strictly on ability he was not a Test-class player, but at no time in his life did he lose that bristling desire to thrash the bowling whatever the state of the game.

Brown is best described as a clumper. He has never been known to stroke the ball away. That is a sophistication beyond his ken. But he does smite it, and he smote it in this match. In forty-five minutes he hit 42 runs, including a six off Mann. The South African spinners at this stage in the innings did not bowl particularly well, but I fancy that their lack of accuracy may have been as much due to Brown's audacity as to any failing on their own part.

Watson produced an innings of 21 that was as rare and cultured as a pearl. During a bad run in a Test series, I have often been referred to as an enigma, but believe me, I can think of nothing to compare with Watson's failures in Test cricket as a source of mystery.

For years Watson has been half a dozen classes ahead of any other left-handed batsman in the country. Technically he looks perfect. His temperament is ideal, and yet he just cannot score runs consistently in Tests. I have no idea why he fails, except that almost invariably he seems to be short on luck, but that cannot be the whole answer.

To make the whole business even more incomprehensible, Yorkshire bounced him in and out of the first team in the 1957 season and in the end let him move to Leicestershire. How a county can afford to treat a batsman of Watson's class in this way is beyond my understanding.

But to continue the story of the Manchester Test. When Hutton and Ikin opened the second innings with England needing 139 to win, Cuan McCarthy made the ball rocket off this rain-damaged wicket. It was the only time I ever saw a fast bowler so eager to bowl that he ran back to his bowling mark.

Ikin, the courageous little Lancashire left-hander, was hit agonising blows about the body. Even in the excitement of this dangerous period, Hutton's ice-cold cricket brain continued to function at its normal tempo. Once when McCarthy hit him on the pad, he flung off gloves and pads, had his leg massaged and then limped around on it before resuming his stance at the wicket. At the other end McCarthy fidgeted and fumed at his bowling mark as five minutes precious bowling time was wasted.

But later proceedings took much of the gilt off this opening partnership. Hutton was on the verge of his century of centuries, and as the innings proceeded it became increasingly evident that he intended to reach that milestone in this match.

On the fifth day both Ikin and Simpson were almost strokeless in their efforts to leave the scoring to Hutton. It was a policy that achieved the unforgiveable and the unforgettable. for it placed in jeopardy England's chances of winning the match. Although the pitch had eased, it only needed one look at the sky to see that rain-storms were not far away, yet still these three went on their precarious way.

Admittedly Hutton was in magnificent form and was taking the game along quickly, but to my mind there can be no possible defence of a tactic which threatens one's own side of victory. After all, we had been playing for the win for nearly four days and to throw it away in the closing hours of the match would make nonsense of cricket as a team game.

Hutton did not get his century, and for his own sake I was glad. At the time this great feat of reaching a hundred hundreds would have been swamped by the controversy that would have raged around it. The method would have supplied ample material for his detractors and arguments about the innings would have gone echoing on through the history of cricket.

Just how dangerous was the policy he, Ikin and Simpson were following was shown when rain drove the teams off the field with England still short of the required runs and Hutton 91. Fortunately, it did not last long and soon after the teams went back on the field Hutton needed six for his century with the game almost over. Slow left-hander Mann sportingly obliged with a slow full toss which Hutton could only hit for four over the top of cover. So he retired at 98 not out with his century of centuries to wait for the Yorkshire match against Surrey at the Oval.

I would emphasise that this method of scoring England's runs was an agreement between the batsmen at the wicket. It certainly did not emanate from the skipper, Freddie Brown. Also, it is my opinion that Simpson and Ikin were as much to blame as Hutton for this misplaced sense of generosity.

Both of them were experienced enough to know that this sort of scheme was out of place in a vital Test match.

In 1951 Athol Rowan was at the top of his powers as an off-spinner, and I shall always consider him a greater bowler than Hughie Tayfield, the man who was so successful against England in 1955 and again on the 1956–57 tour of South Africa.

Rowan had a bounce, spin and hostility off the pitch that Tayfield has never possessed. The assets which have put Tayfield at the top are, I believe, his uncanny, persistent accuracy, his beautifully planned field placings and the outstanding quality of the fielders in those positions. But Tayfield had never possessed the 'flip' off the pitch that is the hallmark to my mind of a great bowler in his own right. As a batsman I know which of the two types I would sooner meet.

While on the subject of off-spinners I would say that the two outstanding men of my time were Jim Laker of Surrey, and Tom Goddard from Gloucestershire. Both these men possessed spin, flight and control to an uncanny degree. Both could make the ball fizz off the pitch like a spinning-top, and even now Laker seems to get better every time I meet him.

Strangely, Goddard, once a quick bowler, never consciously tried to flight the ball. He achieved this side of the art of slow bowling almost by accident. He could move the ball away from the bat, or hold it back, but he was never quite sure how he did it. I remember that the first time I ever saw Denis Compton bat, Goddard dismissed him caught at forward short leg playing at the ball too soon.

After the Test match I went back to county cricket where the form which was to bring me two thousand runs in the season continued. It was a golden summer, 1951, and the hard wickets suited my brand of stroke play.

My display at Manchester had been good enough to keep me in Test reckoning, and when the selectors were thinking in terms of a side for Leeds, their biggest problem was to choose between Reg Simpson and myself. We were both included in the Gentlemen and Players match in what, to all intents and purposes, should have been a straight fight.

Eventually both of us were ousted by Peter May who struck the Players' attack of Bedser, Statham, Hilton and Tattersall for a glorious century and so wrote the introduction to his own Test career.

My initiation into this traditional match, one which I confidently expected to be a solemn occasion, was the sight of Denis Compton shuffling down the pitch to smite the Gentlemen's bowling to all parts of Lord's. With an extraordinary blend of cheek and genius he hit 150 in three and a half hours—and not a chance did he give.

On the second day there came another great innings, this time from May. In his first half hour at the wicket the future England captain scored only two runs, but the caution was justified because his side were on the verge of trouble with both the opening batsmen, Simpson and David Sheppard, out for 53. Afterwards he began to play those incomparable strokes of his in front of the wicket and went on to reach a hundred in just over four hours.

The match was won by the Players with another of those fantastic finishes which has marked this series since the war. The last of the amateurs' wickets fell with only three minutes of play left. As I had collected only 40 runs in two innings, and Simpson 22, I was not greatly surprised when I was dropped from the Leeds Test and May included. Simpson's opening bat place went to Frank Lowson.

May celebrated in typical fashion by making a hundred in his first Test after so nearly being out off the first ball. He lost the delivery from Athol Rowan through the air, pushed forward hopefully and took his first run as the ball ran down to fine leg off the inside of the bat.

I was made twelfth man for the match and fielded for most of it after Trevor Bailey had broken down with a strained back soon after the start. Bailey's back had been suspect for some time and probably now, after this period of years, he would say that he should not have attempted to play in a

43

five-day Test. This was an occasion when Bailey's keenness for Test cricket and his great love of a fight overcame his discretion. In a way I was thankful for the chance to get on to the field for it relieved me of most of the burden of the twelfth man chores.

Frankly, that Fourth Test was a bore. Far too many runs were scored for anybody's good, Over a thousand runs at an average rate of 47 an hour, and inevitably the match was left drawn and the bowlers exhausted. For England, Hutton and May scored centuries and the injured Bailey 95.

South Africa boasted a double century from Eric Rowan, of which I do not remember a shot. It was a colossal monument to his own patience and powers of concentration. It did nothing to entertain the crowd, although the methods Rowan employed could undoubtedly be justified by the responsibilities he shouldered in a side whose main batsman, Dudley Nourse, was still not fit.

Far more memorable in this otherwise dull match, was the innings of Roy McLean. It was the first time this South African hitter treated us to a successful fling, and in view of all that had gone on around him it was a remarkable effort.

His driving sent the ball through the covers like tracer bullets. Malcolm Hilton, the Lancashire slow left-hander, posted four men in the covers whose main job was to trot to the boundary to retrieve the ball. When he added a fifth, McLean promptly lifted him back over his head for six. This champagne cricket ended on a note of anti-climax, particularly for the spectators, when McLean was run out.

Not that I had much sympathy for this Yorkshire crowd. They deserved just about everything they got for they were guilty of the worst display of cricketing manners it has ever been my misfortune to meet in this country. That genial genius Denis Compton dropped Rowan twice after the South African had completed his double century and been batting for nearly nine hours.

The first time was when Alec Bedser came on for a loosening up spell with the old ball and promptly achieved the miraculous by coaxing a comfortable catch out of Rowan for Compton. Denis, probably, had been lulled into a coma by the batting he had been witnessing, and he put it down.

At the time he confessed apologetically—"You don't expect things like that to happen when a bloke has got two hundred and the old ball is being used."

Not long afterwards, five runs before he was dismissed, the same combination of Rowan and Bedser offered Compton another chance which he again missed.

These failures brought howls, catcalls, and jeers from the crowd. After that, every time Compton touched the ball they produced a hooting noise that jarred the ears of every man who has ever played cricket for a living.

Catches have been dropped before without eliciting this kind of behaviour. The root of it, I believe, was the competition that existed between Hutton and Compton at that time for the title of the country's number one batsman. Here was the bright star of the south, the man who was a playboy in comparison with their own dedicated Len, muffing two chances off the only two balls delivered by England bowlers that did anything off that perfect strip. Compton was hot and tired and probably as glum as they were at the pedestrian batting. But he was also a sitting target, and this crowd bayed as they discovered these signs of mortality in a lesser god.

It may be that in some obscure way they thought they were boosting the cause of Hutton. But Hutton was capable of doing his own boosting with his bat. Maybe they thought that the two players, were jealous of each other's prowess. If that was the case they were completely wrong. The relationship between Hutton and Compton was perfectly amicable and normal. Each did his best with the bat and was content with the results. They were rivals only in the sense that both were great players in the same period.

Whatever the motive, Yorkshire spectators did their reputation no good by this outburst.

Earlier in this chapter I called 1951 a golden season for me but it was also tinged with sadness at my brother's retirement from the game he loved. Ken went out on a most spectacular note, with a wonderful bowling performance against our neighbours Somerset, at Taunton in May.

At three o'clock on the last afternoon the scores were about level with eight or nine Somerset wickets standing. It seemed the most certain drawn match of all time, at least until Ken intervened. First he took five wickets at ten runs apiece, picked up three good catches at gully off Sam Cook and then, when Gloucestershire were left to 105 to win in fifty-five minutes, he thrashed an unbeaten 25 and we were home with seven minutes and seven wickets to spare.

And that was the last time he ever played in a first-class match.

The back injury which had troubled him throughout his cricket career, at last put him out of the game. The nearest he got to the county side again was when he had a test in the nets before the county's match against the South Africans.

Ken's ailment really started when he was in the Marine Commandos. He took one or two knocks on the back, and then when he had his week's trial prior to joining the county, he put everything into his bowling with the result that he overstrained himself. He was never really a hundred per cent fit from that time onwards. Practically every medical authority in the country tried to find the remedy for his back.

Between the bouts of treatment he managed to claim for himself a splinter of cricket history by taking all ten wickets with his medium-fast deliveries against Derbyshire.

But for months he tried to bowl at full speed even though his back was strapped and he was in pain. He never refused a skipper's request for "one last effort", even though he knew it would prostrate him after the match. Once against Kent an umpire, Sam Pothecary, suggested to our skipper, B. O. Allen, that Ken was just about all in. Ken had made no complaint, and Sam being the nearest to him as he was bowling, was the only one who knew just what pain he was going through. At the end of that day we had to help Ken off the field.

Some misguided people thought he was making more of

his back than was necessary. In the Army it is called 'lead-swinging'. Before 1951 was very old they were apologising to him, if only mentally.

Ken was a useful cricketer who hit the ball hard and as a bowler moved it both ways off the seam, and he looked a likely successor to all-rounder Reg Sinfield.

Ken's decision to quit cricket was neither sudden nor surprising. His condition had been worsening for some time and in the end he had no real alternative but to finish with the game.

Not that inevitability made the decision any easier. Cricket was the great driving force in Ken's life. As I mentioned previously, he loved it and lived for it. He had never recovered from the pleasant shock of discovering that he was good enough to earn his living at it.

When the time came for him to finish he was in despair. He went back to golf for consolation, improved his game, and now plays some club cricket. He attends occasional Test matches and has a job which earns him a better living than he would have done as professional cricketer. So all in all I suppose it can be said that retirement did him good in that it assured him of a sounder future. But at the time it nearly broke his heart.

CHAPTER FIVE

TOURING ABROAD

A FORTNIGHT after the 1951 season ended I was on my way to India with M.C.C. for my first overseas tour. Looking back, it was not as sensational a tour as some that came later to that country (to start with, *nobody* doused an umpire!), but it certainly did give me a grounding in first-class cricket as it is played in different conditions, And believe me, an Englishman meets so many contrasting conditions on a trip to India that it seems like half a dozen tours rolled into one.

On the journey out Brian Statham, the Lancashire fast bowler, and I struck up a friendship that has lasted ever since. Since then we have shared rooms on every overseas trip. He is a person for whom I have the greatest respect—a great chap and the unluckiest fast bowler of my time. He bowls with almost slow bowler's accuracy, yet he is so often robbed by the ball lifting over the stumps or being deflected by a late snick that sometimes I could weep for him. In foreign conditions, once the shine has gone off the ball, he tries to do nothing more ambitious than bowl straight and fast. His maxim is—"They miss, I hit." This admirable policy was to be confounded by umpiring events in India.

Once we arrived in India we had two days in the nets, after fourteen days on the boat, before our first game. The temperature during our practice periods was hovering around ninety degrees and humid with it. On the first morning I went out to the nets, I gave it up after five minutes. And I like the heat!

Of all the tours I have been on, that to India is the one which needs the most careful vetting by our authorities. In

(*Right*) Walter Hammond off drives —and (*below*) the author in similar pose.

Two action studies of Hugh 'Toey' Tayfield, the South African off-spinner.

the eagerness of the Indians and Pakistanis to see an M.C.C. side, it is too easy for us to get involved in a schedule of matches and journeys that are next to impossible in the heat.

It is necessary, too, to keep a careful eye on the playing conditions for they change like a chameleon. We played first on turf, then coir matting, jute matting, turf again (where water had been poured on the pitch as a protest by the cricket supporters of a neighbouring town), back to jute matting and then on to turf for the Test match. A batsman needs to have an acrobatic technique to survive all these changes.

I scored six of the fourteen centuries made by the M.C.C. Yet the odd thing was that nearly all my runs were made off the back foot on wickets which cried out for forward shots. Wisden said of my batting—"Graveney did well throughout. Hitting six hundreds and scoring over 200 more runs than anyone else, he easily headed the averages. His scoring strokes were generally limited to an arc between extra cover and wide mid-on, usually off the back foot, but he used them well and, keeping his head down, watched the ball closely in defence." So once again my batting had become wedged in a groove, as it has done so many times before and since.

At Amritsar, against Northern India, we bumped into some cricket politics, which were more fun than the cricket. Apparently (and this was the local explanation), the town-proud citizens of Patiala considered it an affront to their dignity that Amritsar should be the scene of the important M.C.C. match. So before play started, they are supposed to have slunk out and drenched the wicket at one end.

Whoever did it or for what reason, the deed was most certainly done. The pitch at one end looked like Old Trafford in a Test match.

The sabotage was only the first part of the comedy. Voluble protestations of innocence followed from every Indian in sight, and so confused did officials become in their efforts to mark out a new pitch, that all the playing period before lunch was lost.

As I scored heavily throughout the early matches and made

a hundred in the last match before the First Test match, I suppose it reasonable to guess that I would have been in the Test side.

Instead I spent the match in hospital with dysentery, listening to it on the radio between bouts of wondering whether I was going to leave my bones in a foreign land!

From this radio-match was born a personal theory. Simply, it is this—Indians do not play cricket as a team game. Such is their temperament and upbringing that they play for themselves, and any benefit which comes the way of the team as a result of their efforts is almost purely coincidental.

In this match at New Delhi, England were put out for a meagre 203. Whereupon India started batting as if they were on a hiding-to-nothing in a timeless Test. Nothing was more obvious than that Merchant was after a hundred. At no time was there any effort to score at even a respectable pace, and when India had passed the 150 mark for the loss of only two wickets, ninety minutes batting produced only 39 runs.

Merchant reached his hundred, as almost everybody knew he would, but still the Indian captain, Hazare, who was at the crease, made no attempt to declare. A reasonable point to close the innings would have been at tea-time when the Englishmen, who had been fielding for nearly two days in the heat, were looking like survivors from a Sahara expedition.

But no. Hazare delayed his declaration until next morning, so giving the Englishmen a night's rest.

As regards this declaration, I think it is not without significance that with his innings of 154 Merchant had established a new Indian Test record. By batting eight hours and thirty-five minutes for an unbeaten 164, his captain promptly relieved him of this honour before declaring.

In the circumstances it was fortunate that only a national record was involved and that nobody mentioned Len Hutton's 364!

By batting most of two days, England managed a draw through the sheer determination of Alan Watkins, the Glamorgan left-hander, who fought for nearly ten hours to hold off defeat. As he had already bowled thirty-one overs, this must go down as one of the great feats of cricket endurance. It saved England, and towards the end of his innings Watkins was literally in a state of physical collapse.

After the Test match we played Pakistan at Lahore and met the tiny Hanif Mohammad. Although a boy between fifteen and sixteen years of age, he batted with remarkable maturity for more than two and a half hours for 26 runs. He was never troubled, never looked like getting out, no matter what Statham, Shackleton, Watkins, Tattersall or Hilton did, and was restricted in his run-making purely through his lack of physical strength in making a shot.

Once again in this match the playing conditions nearly confounded our batsmen. On the first day, when we batted, the pitch was lightning fast compared with anything we had met in previous matches, although its pace faded as the match progressed. In those early stages the pace of Khan Mohammad, the bowler who had played for Somerset, was formidable, particularly when he pitched the ball short. He actually employed a long stop to Jack Robertson, the Middlesex opening batsman, in an effort to make a catch—about the only time I have seen this form of field placing in first-class cricket. The move resulted from Robertson's efforts in the early stages of his innings to hook. Repeatedly the ball sailed off the top edge of the bat, over the wicket-keeper's head for four runs as the ball came off the pitch quicker than the batsman anticipated.

The Second Test against Pakistan was played at Karachi in the most extraordinary conditions. The playing area consisted of a forty yards patch of green in the middle of an outfield of rolled sand. Like a scar in the centre of the turf was the pitch—coir matting on cinder. Between turf and sand was a drop of eighteen inches. And lording it over this strange domain was a groundsman with an old roller pulled by two bullocks.

In these conditions on the first day Khan Mohammad and Fazal Mahmood had the time of their lives. Khan's pace and lift was really pretty terrifying, and Fazal, who was to play such a tremendous part in Pakistan's tour of England, made his medium-pace off-cutters turn back nine inches. Naturally, we found it all rather disconcerting, and were dismissed for 123.

Consolation was not far off though, for Statham let fly at his loose-limbed fastest—still without much luck, for two catches went down—and Pakistan nosed their way in front by 7 runs.

Batting in the second innings was more compatible with a cricket match as the pitch had lost some of its bad temper. I made my second successive hundred against Pakistan and they were left to score 285 to win.

From being a reasonably difficult task against a good attack, this quickly relaxed into being an impossibly easy one. Once the first six l.b.w. appeals had been turned down it became obvious that the Pakistani batsmen were there to stay, short of being clean bowled or lured into giving an incontestable catch. One by one they followed the same pattern of moving back on their stumps, covering them with both pads, and pushing the bat down the line of the ball. That way lay safety and victory.

In twenty-four overs in the second innings, Statham did not take a wicket, yet he grew nearly hoarse shouting appeals as he beat a drum-roll on batsmen's pads. Statham is no cheat, and neither are most English cricketers who gain their livelihood from the game. They are sufficiently experienced at the game to know a reasonable l.b.w. appeal when they see it. Yet not one appeal was granted throughout the innings, although something like thirty were made.

After the match the Pakistan authorities were jubilant at their win, which was understandable. The English bowlers were not so happy, which was equally understandable.

Our over-riding impressions of this match were of the ability of Fazal to take advantage of the least help in the wicket at his pace which was about the same as Alec Bedser, and of the extraordinary powers of concentration of young Hanif, who batted nearly four hours in the second innings for 64.

Another tip which we picked up during this tour was to

check the matting on winning the toss. Sometimes it was left loose, whether by accident or design I am in no position to say, and when that happens batting is a hazardous business.

We returned to India for the Second Test and sampled at Bombay the amenities of the best appointed ground in the world. The hotel where teams stay is part of the pavilion so that the players can walk into the changing rooms in their dressings gowns if they want to. The whole place smacks of luxury, but it has one drawback. Bombay is a dry state, in the grip of prohibition. Those of us who wanted a drink had to sign a form confessing to be uncurable alcoholics! Thus we were allowed four bottles of whisky a month which we kept in our rooms.

The match itself was drawn, but the English performance was on a plane not previously reached on the tour. The Indians made their usual batch of changes for the match. One of the guiding principles in picking a Test side with them is that the local heroes must play. It was an outlook we were to meet to a lesser degree in the West Indies when George Headley and Bob Christiani were included in the Test sides purely on the strength of their local following.

But the Indians had this mass-change system down to a fine art. Not even a century in a previous match was a guarantee of keeping a Test place. The principle also worked the other way for it was a public 'secret' that once Merchant had appeared against England in the First Test and scored a century, he was little interested in playing again.

The England performance was all the more commendable in view of the large score India built up in the first innings. On a pitch reputed to be a little green at the start, Hazare took a quarter of an hour making up his mind whether to bat. When at last he took the plunge, his side rewarded him with 485 runs for the loss of nine wickets.

Hazare completed his second successive Test hundred against us, and in doing so ruined his batting form for the rest of the tour. He tried to hook a short ball from Fred Ridgway, the Kent fast bowler, but pulled the ball on to his forehead and was led away for three stitches to be inserted. This blow shook the batting confidence out of Hazare and from being the lion who regularly mauled England, he became very much a lamb for the rest of the series.

England batted well right through. I scored 175 in eight hours twenty minutes, sustained by a drink and a salt tablet every forty minutes. When eventually I left the crease I felt like my own shadow. But there was no rest and in succession I was fielding and batting again so that out of a possible twenty-seven hours in the match, I was on the field just under twenty-five.

Christmas and New Year, easily the hardest time for an English cricketer to be away from his home, was spent in Calcutta. New Year's day fell during the Third Test, and Nigel Howard, the Lancashire captain, ordered the England side to bed before midnight. It was an order that sprang entirely out of his keenness and determination not to lose the series. But we players were already feeling nostalgic for home, so we retired to our rooms, allowed a reasonable time to elapse and then re-appeared in the hotel in time to see the New Year in together. At midnight Howard was probably the only member of the party in bed!

The cricket in the Third Test was just about the best argument against timeless Tests that I have ever encountered. On this lifeless pitch the match would have been going on now had the clock not intervened on the fifth day. The boredom was relieved only by the fantastic, volatile, noisy people who go to make up an Indian cricket crowd.

The noise they produce is unbelievable. It reminded me of a magnified version of the hub-bub a rowdy class makes when the school teacher leaves the room. Only in India it goes on all day, and is one of the new factors an English batsman has to overcome in his efforts to concentrate.

At a conservative estimate eighty per cent of the crowds know nothing about cricket. They stream into the matches purely in the search for fun and in the hope of meeting people they know.

During the grimmest part of a grim Test match they will chatter, fight and throw bags of flour at each other.

Another disconcerting habit is that possessed by the children of appearing on the field of play. They have the usual child's inquisitiveness about identifying a player without the inhibitions of those in the Western world. A grubby, brown urchin will suddenly appear before a fielder, throw up a precise military salute—a left-over from the British Army days in India—and say: "Meester, meester, name please."

As soon as he is given it, he holds out a dirty hand full of the most violently coloured sticky sweets and the unfortunate fielder has to take one. He has no choice in this matter. To refuse is an insult which would cause indignation all round. Whereupon the boy salutes again and disappears back into the crowd. A fielder who has spent his day on the boundary invariably collects a pocketful of sticky sweets.

Once when Alan Watkins took two wickets in two balls, play was held up while a youngster, holding in front of him an ice-cream cornet, marched solemnly out from the crowd, across the eighty yards of outfield, up to the wicket where he gravely presented it to Watkins. A little confused the Welshman accepted it and then stood clutching the ice cream while the boy marched unhurriedly back.

Being a good cricket tourist, Watkins remembered his rules of play and handed the ice cream to the umpire who put it in his pocket where it dripped away the rest of the innings.

But my most apprehensive memory of the Calcutta Test is the half-completed stand for spectators. Work was first started on it in 1950, but then money ran out and it is still not completed. Now it has become the gathering point for all the wags and jokers who come to watch these matches, and they pack into it and settle down to the business of trying to raise more laughter than the next man. Often their antics and laughter makes the precarious building shake, and I feel certain that one of these days the biggest joke of them all is going to bring building, occupants and their humour tumbling down.

With Calcutta behind us, the series suddenly burst into life with England winning the Fourth Test, India the Fifth and the series thus being left drawn.

At Kanpur we played on a new grass wicket which might be termed Oval-brown in colour. The Indian selectors obviously read the signs correctly for they packed their side with spin, but strangely with leg-spinners, who were not the best bet for a pitch of this type. England brought in Hilton, the slow left-hander, a much wiser choice.

As it turned out the English experience of both batting and bowling on turning wickets was the decisive factor in this match in which the ball turned only at one end. Yet England started the match by taking the wrong route as Nigel Howard spent forty minutes bowling his pace men on a pitch like a stretch of chewing gum. The ball as it pitched at one end made an echoing noise as if the wicket was hollow.

When Hilton came into the attack his first ball turned square, and from then on India were in full flight at both ends. Only Roy defied us, and he held out for over two and a half hours, even though he had probably never known a ball to turn this far.

In this match Hazare, who had seldom looked like losing his wicket before in the series, collected a 'pair'. As I said previously, the blow on the head from Ridgway in the Test at Bombay, seemed to unsettle him, but that was not to say he lacked courage. He was a fine player and easily the best of the Indian batsmen, an opinion he was to strengthen a few months later in England when he tried to rally his side before the terror of Trueman.

Although in the second innings we needed only 76 to win, the game was far from won, for there was still spin bowling of the quality of Mankad, slow left arm, and Ghulam Ahmed, a top class off-spinner, to be overcome. So a policy of aggression was decided on and we got home by eight wickets after losing our first batsman with only 1 run on the board.

At Madras it was India's turn, and they took the chance confidently. Besides levelling the series, they recorded their first Test win—by an innings margin. Perhaps taking a cue from our tactics in the previous Test their batsmen went looking for runs from the start, they fielded with more snap, and Mankad, well supported by Ghulam Ahmed, bowled superbly. In short, India looked like a fighting Test side, and as such reaped their reward.

England lost the match on the first day when, after winning the toss, we allowed Mankad to shuttle us back to the pavilion. His was great bowling in conditions which favoured us. On that wicket we should have been unbeatable, but instead we were in trouble from the time Frank Lowson was bowled with only 3 scored. The Yorkshireman at that time was challenging for a permanent position as an England opening batsman and I must say that in spells he looked the complete answer.

Few newcomers in the past few years have been so complete technically for the job, yet in the final reckoning he missed his chance because he just did not produce the scores to match his promise. Even on those easy Indian batting wickets he could muster only 145 runs in four Tests, and not all those failures can be dismissed on the grounds of bad luck. Admittedly he had his share, twice being the victim in Test matches of bad umpiring decisions. Each time he was given out caught when the fielder took the ball on the half volley. In one case the catcher admitted it afterwards, although why he did not say so at the time was beyond my understanding. It was the sort of thing Keith Miller would have owned up to at once.

Mankad took eight wickets in the first innings purely on the strength of his own guile. I was among his victims, gently brought forward and politely stumped.

When the England innings closed, India fully realised the possibilities of the situation and their batsmen immediately got on with the job of consolidating. They reached 457 before declaring and by that time the pitch was showing signs of wear and tear. So up came Mankad and Ghulam Ahmed again, and down we went.

That was the end of the official tour of India and Pakistan but not, as we soon found out, a time for relaxation. We moved on to Ceylon for what we hoped would prove a quiet game of cricket at Colombo to wind up the trip. We had seen enough of the serious stuff and were in dire need of a rest.

When we arrived there we found waiting for us a Commonwealth side which included Keith Miller, Neil Harvey, Graeme Hole, Fazal Mahmood, Imtiaz Ahmed, Vinoo Mankad and 'Polly' Umrigar. Derek De Sarum, the former Oxford Blue, was skipper. Not only had these celebrated gentlemen been flown in to greet us, but there had been prepared for our pleasure one of the fastest wickets I have ever batted on. One on which the quick bowlers could make the ball fly.

Our gratitude at meeting these conditions after months of batting on the dead strips of India, can be imagined. Not unexpectedly we were outclassed and thrashed. And just to make our discomfort worse, the defeat was administered in heat which seared the eyeballs as it beat off the hard ground. Don Brennan, the Yorkshire amateur wicket-keeper, was actually taken to hospital with sunstroke.

The Commonwealth side batted first and we were impressive neither in bowling nor fielding. I can only plead that we were feeling jaded and just not up to meeting the strongest side that had been put into the field against us on the whole tour. At another time, I feel we would have made use of the conditions, but I doubt if there was ever a real chance of our winning. Miller and Harvey enjoyed themselves, of course, and so did a local batsman named Gunesekara who hit 135 in three hours. But as always it was the mighty Miller who emerged as a superhuman cricketer.

The most successful of the M.C.C. bowlers was a leg-spin and googly man named Tom Graveney, a most underestimated bowler with a masterly control of length and flight. According to his colleagues he is also the collector of the most improbable bowling figures.

When Miller and Fazal started to operate with the ball in these tailor-made conditions, the M.C.C. innings dissolved.

In our two innings there were seven 'ducks', including one from me and two from Jack Robertson, the first time he had bagged a pair.

Such a vibrant, violent cricketer is this man Miller. He would stand out as one of the great personalities of the game in any age. Two incidents occurred in this game which I would class as typical Miller. The first was the six he hit off the off-spin of Jack Robertson, a fabulous carry, the biggest by some distance that I have ever seen. The ball seemed to erupt from the bat.

The second incident was much more personal. I had not scored in my first innings and when I had made one or two in my second, Miller let go a bumper at me. I tried to hook, but the ball only carried off my gloves to the wicket-keeper. A great bellow went up from every player—except Miller. He shook his unruly mop of hair and, waving his hands in that characteristic way, called: "No, no, not out" to the umpire and then went off towards his bowling mark with that long stride of his. The umpire turned down the appeal and I was left at the crease.

Miller, of course, knew as well as anybody that I was out, but he got in his say so quickly that the umpire had made his decision before I even had time to straighten up from the shot and start to walk. Not that the Australian made his gesture out of any feeling for me. It was simply that he had classed me as a possible player against the Australians in 1953 and he wanted to have a good, long look at me at the wicket.

We took revenge for this shellacking that the Commonwealth had given us, on the luckless local batsmen who comprised the Ceylon side. Conditions again suited quick bowlers and Ridgway and Statham romped through them. Again the umpiring was below par and Statham, after having a string of appeals turned down, suddenly broke the leg-stump, whereupon he asked the umpire: "That was bloody close, wasn't it?" This story has whiskers on it and probably the Hambledon men had a version of it back in the eighteenth century, but never before had I spoken to anybody who had taken part in a match when this question was asked. And now I had.

That was the end of the first-class matches. Two more minor encounters followed and then we sailed for home with another season approaching and my prospects of gaining a regular place in the full strength England side bright. My success on this tour had done my future no harm, and at least I knew something about my opponents next summer. They were to be India.

CHAPTER SIX

HUTTON AND TRUEMAN

THE 1952 season will rank among the most vital in English cricket. On one point alone it will ever be a source of argument and controversy, for in 1952 England appointed a professional captain for the first time since the early days. The circumstances of modern cricket forced the change from the amateur captain, and looking back from the comfortable position of five years on, it would seem that the decision was inevitable. But that did not stop it being revolutionary, and there must have been hours of argument and consultation at Lord's before the step was taken.

As it was, the future was to vindicate them, for not only did Hutton build England into a world-beating cricket combination, but he was also knighted for his services to the game.

But in 1952 the appointment of Hutton, or any other professional, was an extreme move. It was made necessary by two factors.

Firstly, ever since the war English cricket had been walking a tight-rope. We shaped successfully enough against the weaker countries, but each time we met one of the stronger Test sides we crashed. The 1950 eclipse by the West Indies had been the biggest shock of all. And as regards our chances against the old enemy, Australia, they were next door to hopeless. The public associated this tradition of failure with the amateur captain. They clamoured for one of the professional stars to do the job, so that the place of the amateur captain could be given to a player whom they loosely described as being 'worth a place in the side'. This outlook naturally concluded that people like Norman Yardley and Freddie Brown were not worth their places—a conclusion with which I would have no truck. Indeed, later, Brown was brought back solely on his playing ability to serve under Hutton against Australia, a selection that would appear to kill any inferences about his ability.

Neither did the public give much thought to the fact that the amateurs generally were fighting their campaigns with sides far inferior to those of the enemy. In fact, with the material at their commands, had they won or even drawn the series of 1948 and 1951–52 they would today be hailed as geniuses. But as far as the public was concerned the amateur captain was an anachronism. They wanted one of the successful professionals such as Hutton or Compton.

Whatever lines the public thought along, it was also evident at Lord's that a change of captain was due. That great fighter Freddie Brown was moving towards the end of a cricket career that, strangely, had shone with more lustre after the war than before it. A replacement was needed, and here was the second main reason for turning to the professional.

No suitable amateur existed for the task of leading England. People like Peter May and David Sheppard were far too young and inexperienced to be put in command of hardened Test teams, although there was always a faction that advised the appointment of Sheppard, the Sussex opening batsman. Modern economic conditions have thinned the ranks of the amateurs. Few players nowadays can find the money and leisure to play cricket for fun.

So Hutton, a quiet man, not given to theatrical gestures, a batsman with a magnificent record for England, was appointed captain of England to great public acclaim. Many were the arguments against his promotion, and mainly they were based on the belief that other professionals would not respond so well to the direction of one of their own number, that Hutton's innate caution would bring disaster, and the responsibilities would effect the flow of runs from his bat. Hutton obliterated the objections one by one, and then went on to establish himself as unchallenged head of the household by bringing back the Ashes for the first time in twenty years. But that lay in the future.

Second only to the emergence of Hutton as captain, was the appearance on the international scene of that chunky piece of fast bowling hostility from Yorkshire, Freddie Trueman.

With his prodigious bowling feats against the Indians, Trueman brought down upon his own head the most extravagant praise from the Press that it has been the lot of any England cricketer to receive in my time. In a way it was understandable.

English cricket had been brought to its knees by the fast bowler. The spin of Ramadhin was all very mysterious, but as far as the public was concerned Lindwall and Miller were the men who had dramatically and persistently humbled our players. So there was this constant search for a fast bowler to give them some of their own medicine, to see if their batsmen liked it any more than ours did. There is no doubt too, that the English batsmen were anxious to have a genuinely fast bowler on their side, for there is less chance of a bumper war becoming out of hand if both sides possess the deterrent, as the politicians say. As a consequence several English bowlers, notable among them Trevor Bailey, were trying to bowl faster than their natural pace with a consequent loss of effectiveness.

There was even one theory, widely held among the elder statesmen of the game, that there would never be another England fast bowler. The argument was that in these times of non-stop cricket it was just not an economic proposition for a man to bowl fast and so lop years off his career. In the light of recent events this theory looks pretty sick.

Anyway, into this charged and controversial atmosphere stalked Trueman, as rough and as tough as granite and full of old-fashioned ideas about bowlers hating batsmen. He had been mooted as the hope of England for some time, but there was never any suggestion that he would make the explosive entrance into Test cricket that he did.

From the start Trueman has never made any secret of his intentions to intimidate the batsmen. He accelerates up to the crease like a runaway train, unleashes bumpers with black browed malice, and glares down the wicket, hands on hips, body tense, at any batsman with the impudence enough to hit him for runs.

All this, combined with wet pitches that made the ball fly, was too much for the Indians. Most of them were out before Trueman started the first stride of his run-up. After playing their cricket on the generally lifeless strips of India, this new menace was altogether too much. As far as they were concerned this was terrorism on the cricket field, and there is still more than one English county batsman who reacts with the same kind of feeling at the sight of Trueman racing towards him.

Hazare and the far less successful Adhikari played him the best among the Indians. Hazare faced each ball with calmness, authority and completely on its face value. To him a long hop did not suddenly change character because it was bowled fast. He established himself as pre-eminent among Indian batsmen, an effort which was all the more worthy in the light of the way his play had deteriorated during the winter's tour after Ridgway hit him with a bouncer. And most of his batting was done at a time when his side were in full retreat.

Apart from Mankad, the rest of the Indian batting was close to being pathetic. I fielded at silly-mid-off to one of their more celebrated batsmen and was astounded that I could actually see the whites of his eyes as he gazed down the pitch at the approaching Trueman. I have never seen a man so frightened.

Hazare must have been heart-broken at the performances of 'Polly' Umrigar, a man who came here with the reputation of being a great batsman. Umrigar decided on a policy of playing Trueman on the move towards the square leg umpire, and was actually bowled at Manchester by a ball he could not reach.

Thus almost overnight the Press found themselves with a new star on their hands, and a fast bowler at that. Not surprisingly they took advantage of their good luck and the news was shouted to the four corners of the world that a new champion had appeared and that English cricket was about to come out of the wilderness. But the ballyhoo was Trueman's misfortune.

I believe that the pressurised treatment in the early part of his career set Trueman back a year or two. From the start he was saddled with an impossible reputation to live up to. He had suddenly become the scourge of the world's batting without sufficient regard having been taken either of the quality of the batting or the batsmen that he had overcome. From 1952 onwards every move Trueman made was watched closely in anticipation of a sensation. Of course Trueman was not that good. No cricketer born of flesh and blood could be.

He fell away in his performance, and had to fight his way back into the England side. There was never any doubt that he would succeed, but I do feel that if he had made a more normal start in 1952 he would have been spared some of the publicity. As it was he was almost too successful for his own good.

Now Trueman is at the top and I say without reservation that he is a great bowler. His pace, hostility, control of swing put him in the top bracket of fast bowlers, and his great heart keeps urging him forward into attack at the end of the longest and hottest day. No batsman I have met enjoys batting against the modern Trueman, and I can think of no greater compliment than that.

The First Test at Leeds early in June provided both men of the moment, Hutton and Trueman, with a grand entrance into their new rôles. Both Yorkshiremen satisfied themselves and their supporters as England went to a seven wickets victory in a match packed with excitement and incident. The game was so pitted with batting collapses and gallant rescues that an account of it must read like a Victorian novel.

Hutton started his tenure of the England captaincy by losing the toss and the Indians went in to bat on a good wicket. But, as during most of the series in India during the winter, their batsmen seemed all too willing to leave the pattern of the game in the hands of the bowlers. They made no attempt to take the initiative and Hutton was too experienced to give them the opportunity. He switched his bowlers about and India lost three wickets for 42.

This situation brought together Hazare and the twenty-year-old Manjrekar and between them they saved their side. Before the series was over, Hazare was to become a past master at batting in this sort of situation. But Manjrekar, an inexperienced cricketer, showed a desire to fight and make strokes that was missing from the play of his colleagues. He was a believer in the calculated risk when batting and had more of the Indian players followed this policy in the first innings they might have won this First Test and so changed the fate of the series, or at least made it less one-sided.

The fourth wicket, that of Hazare's, fell at 264, and then India were on the slide again. Half an hour after the start of play, next day, India were all out for 293. Yet their innings ended ominously, for Jim Laker spun out four men in nine balls after overnight rain had soaked the pitch.

In next to no time after the start of the England innings, England were struggling against Ghulam Ahmed's off-spin. Out went Hutton, Simpson, May and Compton, and then the game changed direction again.

Alan Watkins and I, batting partners on the Indian trip, put on 90. For my own part, I was happy with this innings played in unpleasant conditions against a top-class spinner. There is no more searching test of technique and temperament than that.

Godfrey Evans, that most vital and effervescent cricketer whether behind the stumps or at the batting crease, helped flail England into a 41 runs lead with 66 in ninety-seven minutes.

Then on the Saturday the game exploded with the most astonishing start ever made by a Test side. India, from being favourites to win, slumped into ignominy as the first four wickets fell without a run on the board. Trueman took three of them and Alec Bedser the other, and the atmosphere around the ground must have resembled that of a Roman amphitheatre. The cricket was played in shocked, tense silence, split every few minutes by a great, exultant roar as yet another Indian wicket fell.

Astonishing cricket that it was, it only served to show what a crest Trueman was beginning to ride. Of the four men dismissed for nought, only Gaekwad was dismissed by a delivery that did anything unexpected, and he was caught by Laker off Alec Bedser from a ball that lifted nastily. Trueman dismissed Roy, Mantri and Manjrekar with three very ordinary balls whose greatest asset was tremendous pace.

Roy, a better opening batsman than his scores in England would indicate, was caught at first slip off the back of the bat, hooking at a long hop. Mantri left to a half volley, to which he played back, and Manjrekar pulled a ball into his wicket from well wide of the off stump.

To add to the incredible excitement, Trueman had achieved two legs of a hat-trick, but there was no willing third victim. Hazare came to the crease, made another half century and was finally dismissed when Trueman was brought back for a late fling. Three Indian wickets fell at 143, but that was the last fantastic episode of this gyroscopic game and England were home.

Ten days after the end of the First Test, England and India were at battle stations again, this time at Lord's. Again it was a match of great interest, if lacking the near-hysteria of the previous encounter.

India were reinforced by the appearance of Vinoo Mankad, who was released by Haslingden to play in the Tests and so literally came straight out of Saturday afternoon cricket into the five-day game. He made this transition even more incredible by turning in an astonishing all-round performance.

Opening the Indian innings he scored 256 runs, and then in the rôle of slow left-hand bowler delivered 97 overs. Even now it seems hardly possible that a player could come from half-day cricket into Test matches towards the end of June when the first-class cricketer has played himself into form, and achieve such success.

Mankad went to the wicket with Roy, immediately on Hazare winning the toss again. On a perfect batting pitch without much pace in it, they were a complete contrast in their methods. Roy pushed, prodded and defended suspiciously while the willing Mankad played his league cricket strokes at every opportunity. One of them was quite startling.

Hutton followed his usual policy of making quick bowling changes and before the game was very old, probably about half an hour, he introduced the leg-spin of Roley Jenkins. The high-flung slows of the Worcestershire man were received by Mankad as temptation not to be refused. As Jenkins delivered the third ball, the Indian hared down the wicket and lifted it straight over the sightscreen. I remember feeling a little embarrassed by this shot, and probably a little guilty, too. This fellow did not seem to realise what five-day Test cricket was all about.

He showed a great appetite for the quick bowlers and the new ball, too. He flung his bat at them with great zest as if he enjoyed breaking every canon of the game. His second innings was even better, for he hit 184 in four and a half hours after loosening up with 31 overs earlier in the day! He passed Hazare's Indian record, welcomed Jenkins this time by pulling his first ball for six, and generally had the time of his life.

After the Leeds debacle, Mankad brought realism to Trueman's bowling figures, showing as much partiality for him as anyone else. Yet this cavalier treatment of the Yorkshireman boomeranged on him later in the series as he tried in vain to hook short deliveries on pitches faster than this one at Lord's. In fact, his hooking, so confident and sure at Lord's, became the weak point in his batting armour.

Mankad received the inevitable support from Hazare

and it seemed ill-justice that these two should fight so hard in a side which history will say was swamped by eight wickets.

Young Manjrekar did nothing to suggest that he would repeat his century triumph of Leeds, and despite his subsequent batting failures I maintain that he was easily the best of the young performers who came here with India in 1952. He has the requisite of a good batsman—a determination to stay although there were times when he displayed this essential quality to extremes. More than once I have seen him playing resolutely down the line when numbers nine, ten and eleven have been at the other end and his side's need was for runs. Manjrekar, I think, will be a star batsman when the Indians tour England in 1959.

England's batting hit a high note, even though there were those who claimed that it was not enterprising enough until Godfrey Evans appeared on the scene. There are always those who moan at the tempo of the run-getting, but I would point out that if a side loses a five-day Test through employing three-day tactics, then the captain is guilty of throwing the match away. I agree that stroke makers should be allowed their freedom, that batsmen should not have a game foreign to their natures foisted on them, but to say that all captains should approach Test matches with the object of winning in three days is unreal.

For better or for worse, the whole accent in modern Test cricket is on winning. Get the result in the book is the modern outlook, one with which the public is in full support. I believe that the present cricket fan would rather see his side win than go down to defeat at a gay jog-trot.

In this innings England made a cautious start but justified it by piling up a total of 537. Hutton scored 150, putting on 158 at a run a minute with May, but it was on the third day that the batting, with Godfrey Evans as its inspiration, ran riot.

Evans with his energy and brilliance is a man capable of raising his side to the greatest heights. Conversely, he is just

69

as capable of flooring the opposition by sheer impudence, particularly if they happen to be as temperamental as these Indians were. And at Lord's on the third day he was in his most dazzling vein.

He and I put on 159 together for the sixth wicket in two hours and ten minutes. Evans' share was 104.

From the start it was possible to see that as long as his luck held, Evans was capable of creating history and scoring a century before lunch. He went after the bowlers from the start and shook them by the scruff of the neck until their last drop of confidence was gone. Nobody escaped punishment. Even a master of defensive bowling like Mankad did not know where to pitch the ball to him.

That two hours batting before lunch was like a pantomime. Evans was square cutting from off the leg-stump, sweeping from outside the off, and all the time we were taking ludicrous singles in our efforts to keep the strike with him. Quickly Evans jostled the scoreboard along and slowly the hands of the clock went round, until it became obvious that a century before lunch was imminent.

An over started at twenty-five minutes past one, and during it Evans took his score to 98. When the over reached its end we batsmen stayed at the wicket while the fielders dawdled to their positions. Hazare himself was the bowler, I believe, but before the field could settle into position umpire Frank Chester had the bails off and we were on our way into lunch with Evans robbed of his record.

Some of the crowd booed, mostly at Hazare. There seemed to be some suggestion that the Indian captain had forestalled Evans by wasting time before the last over. In my opinion it was an accusation completely without foundation. Hazare was slow in changing his field, but then he always was. He was a slow-thinking, methodical captain who sometimes became lost in speculation when he was taking part in a game. I think that happened this time as he wandered in from deep mid-off. It is quite likely that he was so engrossed with the problem of stopping Evans' romp that he lost account of the time. But whatever the reason, I steadfastly refuse to believe that gamesmanship effected the issue.

If anything, I rather fancy that both Evans and Hazare were victims of a too conscientious interpretation of the rules. Chester was a magnificent umpire, although he aroused opposition in some quarters because of his flamboyant gestures during matches. In this case I feel he might have allowed another over to start. After six years I am not in a position to argue as to the exact position of the hands of the clock, but I remember thinking as I left the field that Chester had cut his decision pretty fine.

The least disappointed in all the hub-bub was Evans himself. He commented: "Records like these are only for real batsmen," and after the break went out and helped himself to a four off the first ball.

At Lord's, the Indians had put up a reasonable show, but from then on their performance rocketed downhill. As so often happens with a weak side, luck went the other way and in their last two Test matches, at Manchester and the Oval, they were caught on bad wickets after rain. This was the sort of misfortune that used to dog England in the bad old days soon after the war.

The Third Test was a rout. England batted first and from the usual cautious beginning built another good score with a second century from Hutton. Proceedings were more or less sedate and normal until Evans strode out to the wicket again and all India shuddered. Out of 84 runs scored while he was at the crease, 71 came from Evans. He departed like an expensive squib with a two, three fours and catch to the bowler off successive balls.

Whereupon the Indians were herded to the wicket for the slaughter. They were required to bat on a greasy surface which enabled the genuinely fast bowler to whip the ball through, against Trueman attacking with a gale at his back (Bedser was big-heartedly labouring into it at the other end), backed up by English fielding which was nothing short of superlative. All this, plus the odd oath that Trueman threw

71

down the pitch as part of his normal fast bowler's armoury, was too much for the Indians. They scattered.

Trueman finished with the eye-blinking figures of eight for 31 in the first innings. He had a relatively easy time in the second as Bedser and Lock continued the carnage and the poor dispirited Indians were dismissed twice in a day—the only time in modern Test cricket that such a thing has happened.

The England fielding in this match was something to remember with pride. The side just bristled with great fielders, and from the time Tony Lock picked up a brilliant catch from Mankad in the first innings—the first time he touched the ball in Test cricket—they were right on top. Trueman bowled to three slips, three gullies, two short legs and a silly mid-off. Godfrey Evans was possibly the greatest wicket-keeper the game has known, and there were five great close to the wicket-fielders in Jack Ikin, David Sheppard, Alan Watkins, Freddie Trueman and Tony Lock, as well as five other players all of whom were good fielders.

As well as the present England Test team fields, I feel that this was the greatest catching combination I ever appeared with. Not even the most outrageous chance escaped them, and they took all their catches with such ridiculous nonchalance.

I am a great believer in the modern fashion of clustering the young fielders around the bat. It is not so long ago that the older players and the bowlers used to populate the slips on the basis that they would be able to conserve their strength there. But fielding close to the wicket needs a young man's reactions and I think most emphatically it better to see the occasional run lost in the outfield through the slowness of older players, than have a vital catch dropped near the wicket.

I also believe that no matter what his quality as a fielder a bowler should never be placed close to the wicket during his bowling spell. A case in point is Trueman, a world-class fielder when he is not bowling, but extremely human and fallible when he is only among the short legs for a rest period between his own overs.

It stands to reason that a bowler needs to relax between

efforts and a spot where the catches come with the suddenness of lightning is no place to do that. Ray Lindwall, after bowling his heart out in the Lord's Test of 1953, dropped Watson close to the wicket early in the Yorkshireman's innings, and that miss cost Australia the match and possibly the series.

The Indians went to the Oval for the last Test, knowing that their sufferings were nearly over. They managed a draw, but experienced another unhappy time against Trueman and Bedser.

England batted on a good wicket, Hutton and Sheppard amassed 143 for the first wicket, Sheppard went on to hit his first Test century, and the side proceeded leisurely to a total that would appear to have made the game safe. Hutton would have batted on during the second day, but during the interval a deluge hit the ground and turned the Oval into a lake. It seemed impossible that any more play would take place that day, but by five o'clock not only were the luckless Indians being told that play would continue, but that England had declared.

It was a pattern all too dismally familiar to them. As Mankad and Roy walked out to bat, Hutton was clustering his men into the catching positions, and in no time Trueman was at work again. His first ball—nearer him than the batsman—Roy tried to steer off his body and there was Lock pouncing forward like a cat after a mouse to take the catch an inch from the ground. The catching was again magnificent and in no time five of the Indian batsmen were out for six runs. This kind of performance was getting close to the farcical.

Hazare staged his last rescue act of the series, this time with Phadkar for company. There was no play Saturday, and the remaining Indian first innings were almost literally mopped up on Monday morning during drizzle. A downpour in mid-afternoon finally finished the game after Hutton had told Hazare that he expected the Indians to follow-on.

For my part I was not sorry that rain saved these ill-fated tourists from further humiliation. How they must have craved for the sight of the sun and homeland once again. It seemed hard to believe that only a few months before I had been with these people in India when they were celebrating their first Test victory. They had set sail with the usual high hopes common to every touring side and had ended in this morass of despair.

Much of the trouble sprang from the fact that the team was never really behind Hazare. Religious and social problems make the Indian team just about the most difficult in the world to select and lead, and the slow moving Hazare was just not the dominant personality needed to inspire this side in the face of all their adversities.

On the field he fought the side's battle alone, collecting and nursing the worries and responsibilities as if they were precious gifts. Throughout the series I do not recall seeing him consult anyone else on the field for advice. He was prone too, to chase the ball in his field placing. That is, he chopped and changed his fielders, moving them to positions in which runs were taken off the previous ball. For a fielder there is nothing more frustrating and annoying than this policy of futility.

Neither was Hazare completely at ease off the field. Like John Goddard, the West Indies captain, he was not happy at making after-dinner speeches, and it is astonishing how many of these are expected in the course of a tour. When he and his team arrived back in India, Hazare was pushed out of the captain's seat, a spot he was probably not sorry to lose even though the dismissal was harsh in view of the personal efforts he had made on the field to save India's prestige. I saw him again during a fortnight's tour of India in the winter of 1956–57, and even now he is still their best player.

Altogether 1952 was a year full of incident. In August I had a game free, and during that time married Jacqueline Brookman, a Bristol girl whose family had strong cricket connections in Gloucestershire. We honeymooned at the Scarborough Festival, and Jackie sat by and watched as Peter May and I flogged the Yorkshire attack for 187 in quick time for the

M.C.C. In such a manner does romance blossom in a cricketer's life!

Wisden awarded the accolade by making me one of their five cricketers of the year, an honour which was as welcome as it was unexpected. In their appreciation, they wrote: "Splendid as have been his feats, Thomas William Graveney has not yet fully compensated Gloucestershire for the loss of W. R. Hammond, but that he should be likened so frequently to such a master is testimony enough of Graveney's exceptional skill. Undoubtedly no brighter star has appeared in the Gloucestershire cricket firmament since the early days of Hammond himself; some who have played with both believe that with a comparable intensity, almost ruthlessness, Graveney in time could emulate Hammond's remarkable achievements."

This is all very flattering. Yet it is strange how many times my name gets linked with that of Hammond. I can almost believe that it springs from a reluctance on the part of people who saw Hammond to face the reality that his greatness will be seen no more on a cricket field.

Only twice did I see Hammond bat, much to my regret. The first time was in 1939 when I managed to get a day at Cheltenham for the county match against the West Indians. To my horror Hammond was stumped by Sealy off Constantine's slower ball for a score in the twenties (for Hammond to score less than a hundred when I had made a special pilgrimage to see him, was abject failure). I was even denied consolation from George Headley, for that great little West Indian trod on his wicket when hooking a bumper from George Lambert to the boundary like a shaft of light.

After that I wrote it off as a bad day at Cheltenham.

In 1946, Ken and I, crouching among the crowd on the popular side at Bristol, had a memory weaved for us by Hammond. Never shall I forget the treatment the great batsman handed Ellis Robinson, the Yorkshire off-spinner who later went to Somerset. Whenever people use the adjective 'majestic' to describe a batsman, I think of Hammond that day, putting Robinson to the sword.

75

Off three successive deliveries Hammond hit fours. Magnificent strokes possessing the beauty of poetry and the power of a bent bow. Then poor, desperate, mortal Robinson, in his desire to escape further punishment, pitched the next ball almost a yard outside the off-stump. Hammond leaped after it and crashed it over the top of cover with one hand.

This was the cricket version of that boxing saying (attributed to Joe Louis, among many): "He can run away, but he can't hide."

After that I had one more chance of seeing Hammond bat for Gloucestershire, but I refused it. In 1951 he came out of retirement to play against Somerset at Bristol in an effort to boost falling attendances. The crowds turned up all right, but I doubt if they enjoyed what they saw.

Hammond went to the wicket after Emmett and Milton had each scored centuries and sent Gloucestershire off to a blazing start with an opening stand of 193. The great man scraped together seven pitiful runs in 53 minutes. It must have been a cruel sight, but that is something I know nothing about.

I had been out quickly, but I refused to leave the dressing-room to watch after the reports started coming back from other players that Hammond was batting very badly. I had seen him as a great player and that was the way I intended to remember him.

Because of fibrositis in the back—the complaint that put him out of the first-class game—Hammond did not field. It seemed hardly possible that this was the man who had strode the cricket scene like a Colossus.

But enough of sadness, for there was precious little of that about Hammond's play. His name is a legend and it used to fascinate me to hear the stories the older professionals would tell about his batting. They would argue as to which type of attack he relished most, then after coming to the conclusion that he liked them all would qualify it by saying that he had a particular appetite for leg-spin. That type of spin fed his off-side shots.

I am told that Tom Mitchell, the England and Derby-shire player, just could not bowl to him. Once Hammond gave a rocketing, neck-high chance off Mitchell and Les Townsend put this hot handful on the grass. At tea-time the frustrated Mitchell exploded: "I've been trying to get that b . . . . out for nine years, and that's the first chance he's given me."

CHAPTER SEVEN

WEST COUNTRY THOUGHTS

GLOUCESTERSHIRE followed the example of England in 1952 and settled seriously to the problem of sorting out the captaincy problems. By the end of the season the county had raised itself to ninth place in the county championship, an improvement of three places on the previous season, under Sir Derrick Bailey, successor to B. O. Allen.

Yet the position was hardly satisfactory among the players themselves. Sir Derrick would rank among the world's greatest if captains and players were judged on keenness alone. His love for the game was almost fanatical. Yet this very strength was also his weakness, for it meant that he was a great theorist on the game. In my cricket at all levels, I do not think I have met another man whose head was so full of theories. And being a fighter and a man of strong character, he put these theories into practice.

That was where his captaincy went astray. The first essential of any captain who is going to approach the game in the way Sir Derrick approached it, is that he must be an experienced player. Not ordinarily experienced either, but a player grown old and wise in the game.

Naturally Sir Derrick could not fulfil these requirements. He was a young man put in command of a team, some of whose professionals had been playing cricket before he was born. On top of that, although he was a good player, he was not first class.

Towards the latter end of the 1952 season the young professionals in the county made their views known to the committee, and so Gloucestershire started 1953 with a professional captain, Jack Crapp.

But I believe the job nearly went to Donald Carr, who made the trip to Bristol on the suggestion that he might become assistant-secretary to the county. Arrangements were never finalised and Carr eventually joined Derbyshire.

Sir Derrick Bailey's efforts in raising the county in the championship table in what was to prove his last season, was all the more commendable in view of the uncertainty of the composition of his team at the time. 'Bomber' Wells and John Mortimore had emerged as the off-spin successes of the previous season, yet they appeared only spasmodically because of National Service. So who should re-appear on the scene but that Peter Pan of cricket, Tom Goddard, at the distinguished age of fifty-two. He proceeded to bowl more than 400 overs and by taking forty-five wickets proved that retirement had taken none of the destruction from his spinning fingers.

Goddard had gone out of regular first-class cricket in 1951, reluctantly but necessarily after pneumonia laid him low in the spring. He was no youngster to shake off the effects easily and he took only thirty-seven wickets for the county in the season. Yet in more than two decades he had established a reputation as one of the great off-spinners of the game, and he had bided the county over until there were sufficient youngsters of class available to step in and take his place, if not replace him.

As I mentioned in the first chapter of this book, this phenomenal spinner was a medium pace failure at the beginning of his career. He first joined Gloucestershire soon after the Great War and for six seasons impressed nobody as a pace bowler. Whereupon he left the county and became a member of the M.C.C. staff, where he began to develop the spinning trade. Then came one of those strange coincidences. Beverley Lyon saw him turning off-breaks in the nets at Lord's, raved to the Gloucestershire committee about his ability, and in 1929 Goddard was back in the West country. That really was the beginning of his success story, and Beverley Lyon deserves all credit for sponsoring it.

By the time he retired in 1951, Goddard, with his great height that made the ball bounce and his leg-of-mutton hands which sent it spinning towards the leg stump, had taken 2,934 wickets—a prodigious feat that makes a bowler's job seem childishly straightforward.

Goddard was not the easiest of cricketers to get on with, or to get to know. When bowling he was completely immersed in the game and not prepared to suffer fools lightly. When a chance was put down off him, his dismay that the perfection of his bowling and scheming had been marred would manifest itself in a way that was hardly lovable. Goddard was a tough cricketer, a hard cricketer, and because he was these things he was also a great cricketer.

But to the young cricketer feeling his way tentatively in the game, he was a formidable character. A youngster needed to be pretty resilient to shrug off a dropped catch if Tom Goddard was the bowler. Now this huge, black-haired man with the craggy face has mellowed. The cricket pressure is no longer on him, testing the steel in his make-up.

Among those who dominated the bowling crease for Gloucestershire in 1952 was Colin Scott, by turns fast bowler, off-spinner and then medium pace. At medium pace Scott took over a hundred wickets and notched his best season for thirteen years. He had been handicapped by a lack of confidence in his own ability—always pretty considerable—and that proved a bigger threat to success than the knee-injury which retarded his career as a fast bowler.

It is strange how injuries have hit Gloucestershire cricket since the war. Brother Ken was put out of the game altogether, and George Emmett was told that the end of his cricketing days was in sight when he was diagnosed as having the proto-type of a Denis Compton knee. Emmett damaged his right knee while serving overseas in the Army. Specialists told him it was unlikely he would play much more, but George made up his mind and through sheer will power restarted his cricket life and went through the now familiar routine of medical treatment after long days in the field. Not only did his career continue but he went on to gain a Test place and now is captain of the county.

In 1939 Colin Scott was said to be one of the best fast bowling prospects in England. After the knee trouble something went out of his run-up and final body swing so that the late swerve disappeared from his bowling. He had an operation in 1947, but it did not bring the deadliness back to his fast bowling.

Frank McHugh, the six-foot-three-inch fast bowler who joined the county from Yorkshire, was another who was struck down by a lengthy illness at a time when he had found the key to success by cutting down his pace and improving control of length and direction. In his bad old days when one of his deliveries was liable to fly anywhere, McHugh was a bowler always liable to bowl me in the nets. He was so unpredictable, an extreme mixture of good and bad, that I found it hard to concentrate against him as I did against better bowlers.

Arthur Milton is another player who has been hit by injuries at vital moments in his career. Without them I believe he would be an established Test cricketer.

Not in the same category, of course, but even more disastrous from the county's point of view was the skin complaint that helped make Charlie Barnett decide to quit the first-class game in 1949 and take to league cricket. Barnett, the man who had helped me through my cradle days with the county, suffered from eczema on the legs, and it worried him a great deal although I fancy there was plenty more county cricket in him. He joined Rochdale who paid him for playing on Saturday afternoons, double what Gloucestershire gave him for six days a week. In seven years in the league game he earned more than in his entire career with Gloucestershire. So, in the circumstances, he could hardly be blamed for taking the decision he did.

Barnett was a wonderful player. He and Harold Gimblett, the Somerset opening batsman, were out of the same mould. They would stand up straight and give the ball a terrific bang.

If the first ball of the match was a half volley, it still had to go for four. Digging-in was foreign to their nature, and because it was they made cricket a glorious, unpredictable spectacle. Nobody who ever saw Barnett or Gimblett play a big innings will be able to forget the memory. Neither probably, will they be able to embellish it, for cricket has possessed nothing more extravagant than the accomplishments of these two once they were set. To have them both in neighbouring counties was like finding a treasure trove on Southend beach.

There are pictures about of Barnett playing strokes in the most extraordinary upright, old-print style. He seldom leaned over the ball as most modern players do, yet he was the hardest, cleanest hitter of the ball I have ever known. Even though he was not the senior professional, he made it his business to guide and care for the young cricketers and it was he who helped me select my kit when I was first rigging myself out.

For all his sense of adventure when at the wicket, he was one of the few men in the game not to have bagged 'a pair'. When faced with this possibility he generally responded in the grand manner, as happened once at Swansea. He had been dismissed for o in the first innings, and in the second went out to face the first ball from Peter Judge. As it was bowled, so Barnett lunged down the wicket and crashed it for six. Bowlers could always hope to take the wicket of this refreshing man, but it was a hope for which they had to pay a huge ransom once they failed.

In 1948 he might have been a considerable factor in bolstering England's shaky batting against the Australian speed attack, but he was written off as just another of the many failures during that series because, I believe, the England selectors failed to recognise the type of man with whom they were dealing. Barnett was picked for the England side to bat down the order behind the opening pair of Hutton and Washbrook. In those circumstances there was little point in picking him, as almost anybody who knew Barnett could have told the selectors. Barnett, for all his unorthodox outlook, was essentially an opening batsman.

He liked the position, as few men today appear to. Before an innings he actually savoured the prospect of going in first and meeting the challenge of the fresh, hostile bowlers by throwing his shots at that swinging, shiny ball. Just as patently, to bat in any other position irked him and prevented him giving of his best, although he was a good enough team man to bat wherever he was told.

In 1948 with Lindwall, Miller and Johnston scything down our batsmen, it would have needed something incredible to have stopped the advance of that tremendous Australian side. I fancy that Barnett at number one might have supplied it.

A vintage Barnett innings, the ball bouncing off the bat with gusto, would have boosted the morale of the following batsmen as few things else that series did. And at that time, I believe the psychology of the team was almost as important as its composition.

But the fashion in opening batsmen is for tough cricketers loaded with concentration, who hoard their runs. When a brilliant exception like Barnett is available, the selectors generally decline to take the chance on failure that style of play must always court. From this distance of time, such a chance would not seem to have been outrageous in 1948 when successes were rare among English batsmen. Still, I suppose this is another case of distance lending enchantment. Team selection at the time could have been no picnic.

Barnett, incidentally, was the worst player in the nets I have ever seen. At my first sight of him I could hardly believe my eyes, but without a challenge he could not get interested in the game.

I think a summing up on his career would read: A wonderful player who remembered that cricket was an entertainment. Had he been able to curb his play he would have had a long Test record. But he would not have been Charlie Barnett.

CHAPTER EIGHT

THE GREEN CAPS DOFFED

THROUGHOUT the winter of 1952–53 the conversation topic was on the same universal theme wherever cricketers or cricket followers met—the Australians are coming. Those baggy green caps that bring such vibrant life to our grounds were being greeted with the usual mixture of fear, respect and 'we'll-give-'em-a-hell-of-a-hiding'. These Australians are wonderful people the way they regularly revive English cricket which, before their appearance, is either dying or dead according to the optimism of the speaker.

Somewhere down there, 12,000 miles away, Miller and Lindwall were loosening up and overhauling their thunderbolts, while we sat here in the cold of an English winter waiting and wondering. The public, generally hopeful of an English success in the series, despite twenty years of evidence to the contrary, were even more so this time. England, they said gleefully, were going to meet speed with speed, bumper with bumper, batsman's blood with batsman's blood. The avenging angel spoke with a Yorkshire accent and was named Trueman.

The more discerning, among them most cricketers, tempered their optimism without reaching the pessimism of that ever-present section of the community who crowed: "The Aussies will give this Trueman stick." Which just goes to show that you cannot please all of the people all of the time.

Most of the cricketers of my acquaintance were agreed that Trueman was a great prospect, but we would all liked to have seen him operating against more formidable opponents than the Indians. We were inclined to think that he might prove too inexperienced to be thrown in against these battle-hardened, successful Australians and that a mauling from their batsmen at this juncture might adversely affect his whole future. Against this could England possibly afford not to play their only genuinely fast bowler since the war and the man who had done more to win the Indian series than the rest of us put together?

Compared with answering that problem, the task of consolidating my Test place seemed a minor issue.

Ultimately, of course, the puzzle ended up in the lap of the selectors, and they did a first-class job of solving it. They established as their main principle Trueman's worth to England as a fast bowler of the future, and then set about safeguarding this long term view with their own selections. They kept him out of the first four Tests amid much tub-beating and cries of "we want Trueman", brought him in the last Test and then sat back while England won.

Selectors are fair game for everybody to shoot at, but they certainly deserve all credit for their handling of Trueman in 1953. I should hate to have owned any of their names though, if Trueman had bowled well at the Oval (as he did) and we had lost the series!

All the talk about fast bowling had the effect of altering my batting style yet again, before I even picked up a bat for the new season. Everybody kept telling me how I would have to get right behind the ball to counter this new, extra pace, so that when the new season started I automatically stepped right behind the line of flight to play my shots, making a fetish of putting my body between ball and stumps. The outcome was that the thing got out of hand. I started going too far across the wicket and, as a result became almost solely an on-side player.

By mid-July I was never anywhere near the position for hitting the ball through the covers, my favourite shot. My batting felt peculiar, unnatural.

But at least my new style proved effective against pace.

Miller gained my wicket with an off-spinner, at Manchester when I tried to hit him back over his head, but not until the Fourth Test at Leeds did I fall to genuine pace. And then not until after I had scored a half century in the first innings when it had accounted for almost everybody else, too.

In terms of hard facts, this exaggerated technique was a success because it earned me a place in all five Tests against Australia, a feat achieved by only five other English players in the series—Len Hutton, Denis Compton, Trevor Bailey, Godfrey Evans and Alec Bedser.

Yet if the selectors had asked for my views about myself before the Fifth Test, I should have said that I was not batting well enough to play. I was not asked and I played, badly too, but I was in no position to go to the selectors and ask to be dropped. My international career was uncertain enough as it was, and to have pulled out of the match which was to decide the Ashes would have brought fresh howls about my lack of big-match temperament. In this case the term would have been a euphemism to disguise the belief that I had 'funked' the match. A howl like that might have put me in the wilderness for years.

All the same, by the end of the series I could not hit a shot. At the Oval, Lindwall bowled me a half volley which I hit full off the face of the bat, wide of cover. He strolled across and picked it up. I was nearly heartbroken.

Ironically, while I was in no sort of batting shape for Test cricket, Peter May was dropped and he was not brought back until the last match of the series.

This was a classic case of dropping a class player, a step which to my mind has little to commend it. I thought it evident then that May was going to be one of the great players of the game, and I should have thought it policy to have persevered with him. He was shown the door on the strength of his failures against the Australian bowlers both for Surrey and England.

The facts of the two cases are these. At the Oval he was subjected by Lindwall to an over which, according to Alec

Bedser, was the most fearsome he had ever seen delivered from that devastating bowler. May was truly grilled in what was obviously a deliberate attempt to push him out of the Test selection, and after being beaten repeatedly, departed caught Tallon bowled Lindwall o. Yet this happened in only the second week of May on a pitch which helped quick bowlers, so surely an English batsman could be excused being in difficulties against this class of attack so early in the season? Lindwall gave me enough trouble in August, and by then I had been seeing the ball for four months.

In addition, I imagine that if a list was compiled of England batsmen who were dismissed for o or only little more on their first meeting with Lindwall and Miller, it would include such players as Hutton, Compton, Sheppard and Simpson, so May would appear to have been in good company.

Nevertheless Peter May went into the First Test at Nottingham and was caught behind the wicket, this time off topspinner Jack Hill, in semi-darkness that brought play to an end a few minutes later. This part of the May case needs no arguing—cricket was invented to be played in the sun, not at night.

After that match May and Reg Simpson were replaced at Lord's by Freddie Brown and Willie Watson. Not until the Fifth Test was May brought back after playing what I have been told was a very good century at Lord's. He was particularly severe on the Middlesex fast bowler Alan Moss.

He picked the right place to put on this display for Lord's is recognised as a good setting to score runs if you have designs on an England place. Not only are the selectors there but the Press as well, and publicity, of the right kind, helps as much in cricket as anywhere else. You can score all the runs you like in Taunton and nobody outside Somerset would know how to pronounce your name.

But I shall never cease to be mystified that a batsman of May's calibre was dropped for three matches against Australia in 1953.

The Australians opened the season with their usual victory

march round the counties, building up the old reputation of invincibility, so that one began to wonder if that solitary England win on Brown's tour of Australia really meant anything after all. Yet they started off on a note that soured their chances of success. In an inconsequential thirteen-a-side picnic match at East Molesey in Surrey, Bill Johnston, their utility bowler, wrenched a knee, brought closer the end of his career, and put Lindsay Hassett in a position of despair later on in the tour when it came to finding a spin bowler to capitalise on wet wickets. With Johnston fully fit and a regular member of the side it is possible that 1953 would not have been such a memorable season for England.

The most devastating hint of Australian power came during six days in May when they beat both Yorkshire and the champions Surrey by an innings and a handy run margin. Hassett, leathery little humorist and charming man that he was, was obviously as capable of winning matches as was the clinical and ruthless Bradman. Possibly he made defeat a little more acceptable than did the Don.

The first hint of any slowing down in the Australian tempo came when they played their first representative fixture—against the M.C.C. at Lord's. The match was drawn and it was then, I think, that we had the first concrete evidence that bowling was going to dominate the series and that batting for both sides was to be a hazardous business.

The formation of the M.C.C. side followed the usual pattern. The probable Test bowlers were left with their counties and the Test batsmen assembled to have a look at the Australian bowling. As in most things in cricket this is a policy open to argument. One school of thought says field the strongest side against the Australians on every occasion, get them on their backs and keep them there. That way lies success. I wonder.

Whatever the point of view, the probable England batsmen were shuttled in and out in the first innings to their own chagrin, and the second line bowlers created havoc among the Australian batsmen. So much for theories.

After the Saturday had been lost through rain, the M.C.C. batsmen quickly found themselves in trouble against Lindwall. Neither of the opening pair, Reg Simpson and David Sheppard, scored and Denis Compton collected only 2. These dismissals illustrated one of the prize assets of Lindwall's attack. Compton and Simpson had seen as much of his bowling as most people in the world, yet he was always capable of dismissing them for next to nothing, particularly when there had been a lengthy break since they last met. Lindwall was not a bowler you could ever get to know.

The damage that Lindwall started was completed by Doug Ring, bowling leg-spinners. I was among his five victims and M.C.C. were all out for a miserable score of 80.

If the match had ended there, it would have done no more than boost the Australians already high morale. But they had to bat and when their first four wickets were down for 26 there was even some speculation as to whether they would reach our score. To this dire situation they reacted in typical Australian fashion, one which I believe is in marked contrast to the English attitude, and launched an attack on the bowlers. They hit savagely, often hopefully, yet so successfully that in the end they gained a 99 runs lead.

The lessons of the M.C.C. second innings were scarcely new. We learned that Denis Compton could handle the Australian attack and that Trevor Bailey could defy it with that wet-flannel forward shot of his. This Bailey innings of three hours forty minutes for an unbeaten 64 was a foretaste of his match-saving effort in the Second Test on the same ground. Throughout the series Bailey, with his one shot and air of dedication, was the man the Australians could never really be sure of getting out. By the end of the tour most of them, with Miller the prize example, were prepared to run up and down walls at the mention of his name.

For my own part I saw nothing more of the Australians until the First Test at Nottingham in June, a match that will ever be etched on my memory as Bedser's own. This whole series saw 'the big fella' at his greatest, and I am tempted to ask: Was there ever a greater fast-medium bowler than he? Could there have been?

Maurice Tate fans must take their turn in the queue to answer. I did not see Tate, but I did see Bedser pass the S. F. Barnes record of 189 Test wickets for England. I did see Bedser bowl all day in the hot sun, dragging what small help he could from the impossible conditions. I did see him sending in-swingers ducking in late against batsmen's pads, and then next ball whipping his leg-cutter away from the bat like a fast leg-break. I saw Bedser do all these things at a time when he had virtually been carrying the England attack on his broad shoulders for years, yet he never flagged, nor lost control or hostility. Bedser was not only a giant among men, he was a giant among bowlers.

This Nottingham Test was almost typical of his work. To start with, England went into the match with only four first-line bowlers, including Bailey who opened the attack with Bedser. As far as Bedser was concerned, that kind of decision was like sentencing him to hard labour.

And there he was with his seventh ball thumping the middle stump and sending Graeme Hole back runless. Bedser bowled Hole again in the second innings and thus ended the Australian experiment of playing this young man, a protégé of Bradman's, as an opening bat. His high, curly backlift was eminently unsuited to cope with the controlled swing of Bedser.

At the end of that first day, shortened by rain and bad light, the Australians were 157 for three and all the wickets had gone to Bedser, including the dangerous Neil Harvey for 0. At lunch on the second day they were 243 for four with Hassett still there, his ninth Test century in the book, and the signs apparent that an ominously large total was on the way. Yet they were all out for 249. That was Bedser with the new ball after lunch.

He just swept the batting aside. Hassett, who had played in masterly fashion, was bowled by a ball that pitched on the leg stump and hit the top of the off. He looked flabbergasted at his wicket before he realised what had happened, then called "well bowled" to Alec before moving off to the pavilion.

As magnificently as Bedser bowled in this match, it did not exceed the quality of the English fielding which was of a standard to have made even the heart of Bedser forgive all those catches that had been dropped off him over the years. Evans, behind the wicket, made a catch off a leg-glance by Ritchie Benaud, executed with the full face of the bat, that was quite plainly of the 'impossible' variety. That was a wicket to Bailey's credit, though I fancy Evans should have got into the bowling analysis on the strength of it.

Reg Simpson took another schoolboy fiction catch when he ran from mid-on to mid-wicket as hard as he could with his head down. The next time he looked up to sight the ball it was falling behind him, so he stuck out a hand to take the catch behind his back.

Unfortunately for England the good bowling and fielding did not end with Australia's first innings. We were in dire danger of following on until Bailey closed up shop. Wardle hit cheerfully, and the Australian lead was brought down to 105. Even so this was scarcely a position from which England could expect to climb into a winning position, yet we did, and in the end only time lost through rain robbed us of victory.

Bedser was the man of the hour, taking his wicket harvest to fourteen for the match. Yet he was aided by a classic misunderstanding, which had the Australian batsmen performing in a Sunday afternoon party match spirit. Alec was altogether a handful in the dismal conditions, and as the batsmen proceeded cautiously there was considerable discussion in the Australian dressing-room about appealing against the light. At the fall of the next wicket, Tallon was about to make his way to the crease when Hassett called to him: "Give it a go, Don," meaning appeal against the light.

But during the discussion Tallon had not been listening as he wandered off into a world of his own. He interpreted the instruction as meaning attack the bowling, and obediently took the message to the crease where he proceeded to launch an outrageous assault which sent the ball soaring to all parts of Nottingham. The rest of the Australians took the hint from the happy Tallon, and before an astonished Hassett could intervene, his side were all out.

So after varied alarums and excursions the First Test ended with England well on top. Despite the rain it turned out to be a fine game. Indeed, all the matches against Australia in the 1953 series were more exciting and entertaining than the usual run of five-day Test matches. They were fought razor-keenly by two sides which, although suspect in certain respects, were still of high quality. But the motive force behind them was England's ambition and the last ditch determination of a Bradman-less Australia not to be pushed from her pedestal.

So, after Nottingham, the scene was set for what was to become known as the 'Terrible Test' at Lord's. The early stages of this game gave little indication that it was going to come close to turning the whole population into nervous wrecks. Australia had a bigger opening batsman problem than England who, at the time were giving an extended run to Worcestershire's Don Kenyon. So Hassett, a selfless captain, promoted himself and promptly established a claim to be among the best opening batsmen in the world at the time.

He scored a century against us in the first innings at Lord's which was as fine and controlled as any you could want from a captain trying to build his side's innings. He possessed a calm temperament, a faultless technique, and he was never in any trouble against us until he was dismissed. As with all good batsmen, he had so much time to play his shots.

He and Arthur Morris put on 65 for the first wicket which, as this was the biggest opening stand against England since 1948, is a good indication of the way fast bowlers have dominated post-war Test cricket. By the end of the first day the Australian position had deteriorated to 263 for five. Much of the trouble was brought about because Hassett retired with cramp towards the end of play and so allowed the bowlers a look at another new batsman. Next day Australia were all out for 346, a score not as formidable as it might have been, but still big enough by present day scoring standards.

By close of play that night England were 176 for one after losing Kenyon at 9. Hutton and I had put on 168 for the second wicket. Hutton produced a hundred in this innings which drew ecstatic comment from those privileged to see it. It was one of the great innings of Test cricket, played by a captain who had dropped three catches and seen his opening partner give himself out when none of the Australians appealed. Kenyon walked out after playing the ball into the leg-trap off Lindwall, explaining that he knew he had given a catch and the way he had learned the game, a batsman walked when he knew he was out.

I cannot praise too highly the way Hutton rose to the challenge that was presented to him. When he had been committing his fielding errors—he had a nightmare day in which the ball would not keep away from him—some of the crowd had cheered ironically when he stopped the ball. It was a cruel gesture to a man who carried England's batting until it wore him out.

Both of us played our shots from the start of our innings. We made a point of taking the initiative from the bowlers and the runs flowed reassuringly. I have only one regret about our stand. It is that we scored only 34 runs in the last hour. At twenty five to six Hutton came down the wicket to me and said: "See it out. Mustn't lose a wicket tonight." So we played carefully at a time when the Australian bowlers were flat-footed with exhaustion and finding it hard to bowl a length to us. It was a dreadful waste of a chance to round off the day with a flourish of boundary strokes.

Hutton spoke to me on another occasion during this partnership. It happened when Bill Johnston pitched the ball wide of my off-stump and I put my foot across and drove the ball square with a crossbat. It went for four like a golf ball flying off the tee. I had never attempted the shot before, and I burst out laughing at the result.

Down the wicket the stony-faced Hutton called: "Shut up and get on with the game."

It was a good example of the difference in our approaches to the game.

First thing next morning I was out, as I was at the start of a new day at Leeds later in the series. Immediately the cry went up that Graveney is a bad starter, and Neville Cardus (who should know better) suggested that I should put my alarm back an hour so that I was properly awake by the time I reached the wicket. I cannot think of any reason why I should be more fallible in the morning than at any other time. I always have a net so that I am attuned to the game.

At Leeds I actually did not see the ball that beat me until after it pitched. During that match Bill Bowes, the former Yorkshire and England bowler, came to the dressing-room and suggested that at the start of play I should not lift my bat so high, cutting down my strokes until I had become accustomed to the pace of the wicket.

How the ball from Lindwall bowled me at Lord's, I have no idea. It was a yorker which I hit very hard indeed, making a noticeable mark on the bat, but still it got through to the stumps.

Eventually England crept in front on the first innings, but Australia soon wiped out the lead and by means of another good total—including an untypical, but vital century from Miller—set England the task of scoring 343 to win.

In no time we were three wickets down for 15 runs, and the stage was set for the most dazzling recovery in the history of modern Test cricket. Lindwall took the wickets of Hutton and Kenyon, and then I tried to take my bat away from a ball by Bill Johnston, but it lifted suddenly and carried off the face of the bat to a position between first and second slip where wicket-keeper Langley arrived like a bouncing rubber ball to take the catch. So I returned to the balcony to watch out the rest of the match in an atmosphere that became more and more unbearable.

Watson and Compton were at the crease for the start of

the last day. The presence of Watson emphasised my point that fast bowlers should not field close to the wicket during their bowling spells. On the previous evening a tired Lindwall dropped Watson in the leg-slip area off Ring, although only one person I know of thought at the time that the error would make any difference to the result.

That one was Henry Sayen, an American who played for Gentlemen of England in 1909 and for Philadelphia. He has written a book on the game, and is a man of rare optimism. He declared to the dressing-room in general: "I will give you five hundred dollars if you win." Apparently it never entered his head that we might lose the game, only that we could win it.

After the Lord's Test he would suddenly arrive at Test matches anywhere without prior warning. It seemed to be simply a case of climbing into a plane and arriving in time for the start. He turned up in Sydney and again in Kingston, Jamaica, when we needed to win the last Test to draw the series with the West Indies. Most of the players were a little fed up at the time, after what had been a taxing tour, yet Henry Sayen greeted us with the prediction: "You'll win it O.K. I have never seen you chaps lose." And then he took us all out to dinner and during the next five days we kept our private unbeaten record for him.

But at Lord's in 1953, Mr. Sayen's optimism rather resembled the cheerful drunk who got put in the condemned cell by mistake. As the day wore on, so we players paced up and down the dressing-room reluctant to watch, unwilling to hope, and knowing all the time that a couple of overs could finish the match at any time.

No man can command enough superlatives to pay tribute to this stand of Willie Watson and Trevor Bailey, an epic achievement. They were two contrasting players, yet they submerged every instinct in their desire to save the side and they succeeded.

Bailey found the situation a likely backcloth against which to exercise his talents. The Essex amateur is a batsman of limited ability, yet he is incomparable for rising to the dramatic occasion. The better the opposition, the better Bailey drops forward into his defensive stroke. His is the complete triumph of temperament over technique and a complete refutation of the argument that defensive cricket does not win a series. The Australians could not get Bailey out, and England won this series.

Watson, on the other hand, is a stroke player possessing all the delicate shots in the game. His record would hardly have suggested that here was a man who was virtually going to stay at the wicket for most of the day, defying a rampant Australian side with a self-imposed code of rigid discipline. I think it was the ability to buckle down to a game that was foreign to his nature that made Watson's effort such a great one.

As the pair moved inexorably through the new ball period, so we dared to think in terms of a draw. Then all of a sudden we were facing defeat again.

After nearly six hours at the wicket Watson was out, the victim of tiredness as much as Ring the bowler. Soon afterwards Bailey momentarily forget himself and tried to drive. He was caught at cover. Our hopes depended on Freddie Brown and Godfrey Evans, and I defy anyone to name two batsmen guaranteed to have a worse effect of our already twanging nerves. These two played the only way they know. They hit at the ball, skied it, sliced it, but stuck to their normal pattern of bold batting knowing that if they tried to emulate Watson and Bailey their wickets were forfeit.

The fear that haunted our dressing-room during the last minutes of the match was that Hassett would take the new ball and turn Lindwall and Miller loose on our rumbustious pair. With muscles taut we waited and watched as each over passed, knowing that Brown found Lindwall an almost insoluble problem. But Hassett kept his moderate spinners going and we could hardly believe our eyes. Evidently he reasoned that his fast bowlers would use up too much of his dwindling time, but I fancy it was a false argument for three overs of fast bowling might well have smashed the England

(*Above*) England's past and present captains caught in concentrated mood. Peter May forcing away a ball from Johnny Wardle while Len Hutton crouches in the slips. Freddie Trueman is the other fielder and Tom Clark the other batsman in this shot of a Surrey *v*. Yorkshire meeting.

(*Below*) Tom Graveney returns to the pavilion after his magnificent innings of 258 against West Indies at Trent Bridge, 1957.

Two Gloucestershire favourites . . . (*Above*) Tom Goddard, the off-spinner, bowling for England against South Africa, First Test at Johannesburg, 1939 . . . and (*left*) Charlie Barnett watches the ball speed towards the leg boundary.

innings. As it was, the slow bowlers scarcely justified his confidence for they were not impressive in conditions in which a pair like Lock and Laker would have been unplayable.

Brown, incidentally, was chairman of selectors when he was chosen for this match, and there was considerable speculation at the time that his inclusion would cause embarrassment to Hutton. As far as I was aware this was not the case. Brown fitted in well with the team, was no more prominent in the dressing-room than any other player, and offered his advice to Hutton only when Len asked him for it.

After Lord's, the Australians went to Bristol where George Emmett showed their attack less respect than did a lot of current England batsmen. He smashed their bowling for an exhilarating 141, and probably handled it as roughly as anyone had done for years.

CHAPTER NINE

A STIRRING SERIES

MANCHESTER, dear wet, grimy, dreary Manchester where
Test matches seldom get finished and cricketers need webbed
feet. It lived up to its music hall reputation—which Man-
cunians loyally claim is unjustified—and sprinkled rain on
us on most of the occasions we had the temerity to leave the
pavilion.

Yet before this match had ended in the ninth successive
draw between these sides on this ground, the old bogy of
the Australian fear of sticky wickets had again been blown up
to giant proportions. Most of the game was a tribute to the
tenacity of the people of Manchester in wanting to watch cricket
in such miserable weather conditions.

Play on the first day began at ten to three and might have
produced an Australian collapse but for a rare wicket-keeping
error by Godfrey Evans. With Hassett, Miller and Morris out
of the way, Neil Harvey touched an easy catch to the wicket-
keeper who, in his jubilation, tried to throw the ball into the
air before he had collected the catch. Harvey went on to a
century and then was taken by Evans off a much harder
chance, leg-glancing.

On the second day the spectators received ninety minutes
of water-splashed cricket for their money. By tea-time the
ground was under water.

The start was delayed for half an hour on the Saturday
morning and then the bowlers proceeded to enjoy themselves
on a pitch off which the ball capered spitefully. The Australian
innings ended, England's started, and with it trouble. Not

for the first time Hutton and Compton gave us all a lesson in how to bat in these conditions, and from being in a position to attack Hassett and his spinners were turned on to the defensive.

On Monday the weather returned to normal and there was no play and on the fifth day there was none until after lunch Buying Test tickets in Manchester is a pretty hazardous business, I should imagine.

Yet as it happened, there was reward in store as the Australians found themselves caught on a genuine, snarling sticky dog towards the end of the game. There was never any possibility of a result, yet Hutton kept us going full out as he strived to open up a crack in the Australian morale for future games.

His bowlers—Alec Bedser, Johnny Wardle and Jim Laker (bowling after pain-killing injections in a torn leg muscle)—obligingly presented him with eight Australian wickets for 35 runs. By the time the end of play was reached the baggy green cap had lost its authority as its owners were bewitched and bemused by the ball that turned quickly and lifted viciously.

And make no mistake about it, this was no case of batting made careless because the outcome of the game was settled. These Australians genuinely had no idea how to play the turning ball. They careered down the pitch, playing strokes that were a travesty for the conditions, and all the time the Englishmen kept at them, remembering that there were two more Tests to play and there was no telling what the result of this excursion into panic would be.

Quite the best Australian batting came from the left-handed Alan Davidson. He stayed half an hour but would have gone before had I not got in Hutton's way when he put up an easy catch.

As far as England's bowlers were concerned the pitch was perfection. The sun was on it and the turf was drying. Hutton kept Bedser on until he had claimed his hundredth wicket of the season, and then replaced him immediately with

99

Wardle. By pitching the ball up to the bat where the Australian bowlers had delivered short of a length, Wardle took four wickets for seven runs. His reward for that piece of bowling was to be dropped for the next Test, when a fit Tony Lock was preferred.

So for all its gloom, Manchester provided England with a great morale booster. And from then on the Australians paled every time they felt a spot of rain on their cheeks.

So to Leeds cock-a-hoop, only to find trouble for England. It started when Lindwall bowled Hutton in the first over after Hassett had taken the controversial course of sending England in to bat, and I was on my way to the middle to face the third ball of the match. And what a day for graft, it proved. In heavy cloudy weather with the ball swinging about like a boomerang, the Australians launched at us Lindwall, Miller, Davidson and Archer. These four gentlemen enjoyed themselves far more than did the batsmen.

My contribution to a woeful innings total of 167 was a half century ground out in four hours. I eventually fell to the second new ball after a knock which, in the conditions, was of more importance than some of my more glamorous efforts.

Meanwhile the England dressing-room was like a casualty clearing station. Willie Watson was struck on the foot, a blow all the more painful because it brought about his dismissal. When the ball struck him—it was a full toss incidentally, dangerous in that thick atmosphere—there was a shout for l.b.w. As this was being turned down the ball rolled into the stumps. In addition, Reg Simpson received a blow on the elbow, Denis Compton nursed a bad hand and Trevor Bailey twisted a knee. Liniment flowed like wine during this match.

All one can say about the Australian batting is that they did not hit us as hard as we feared they might. Nevertheless, a lead of 99 in the sort of scores this series producing, was formidable enough. Back came England with one of our by now famous last ditch stands that produced an innings of outstanding courage by Compton who rallied the side, even though his left hand was so badly bruised as to be almost useless.

In the end the Australians were left to score 177 in five minutes under two hours to win. But none of these matches, apart from Nottingham, was destined to end on a normal note. High drama kept interrupting.

It happened here when Hutton tried to cash in on the panic caused among Australian batsmen at Manchester. There was a little help in the Leeds wicket for the spinner, and Hutton took the almost unheard of step of opening his attack with a spinner.

Tony Lock had been brought into the side in place of Wardle, and he was handed the new ball. And straightaway the Australians, particularly left handers Morris and Harvey, hammered him. Lock did not bowl well. He pitched short of a length, probably through trying too hard to spin, and in nine incredible minutes 20 runs had been scored.

They thundered on, these Australians, until there was scarcely a person on that ground who did not think they would win. It was then Hutton switched on the leg theory and England were saved.

Trevor Bailey, the arch wizard of defensive cricket, came on to bowl outside the leg stump, Graeme Hole, going well, swept a catch to me at long leg, and the gallop ended in full flight.

Immediately stumps were drawn the inquest started. Hutton had drawn the game, but was he right to use leg theory, the bowling method that was bringing sleeping sickness to the game? Some critics reckoned England should have gone down gallantly attacking, though their voices were hard to hear in the general sigh of relief that swept the country at our escape.

My own views on the subject are quite definite. I have no affection for leg theory. I feel it makes a travesty of the game, yet as with all generalisations there have to be exceptions and I feel this was one.

From the start of the Australian second innings Hutton

could have played safe. He could have set orthodox fields to his pace bowlers and let the game die a natural death with nobody unduly perturbed. Instead, he played attacking cricket, took an outsize risk on losing, and turned the Fourth Test into a match to be remembered. Having made his bid in circumstances which most captains would have ignored, I feel that he was fully justified in taking every measure to save the game when he saw it galloping away from him. After all, if a man who plays attacking cricket is deprived of the means of remedying his errors, then he is placed in an invidious position.

On some other occasions when Hutton employed leg theory I thought he was wrong. This was not one of them.

On 15th August, there began at the Oval, that typical London ground with its chirpy Cockney atmosphere, the match that will always rate as the most memorable of my life. England won the Ashes for the first time in twenty years and the nation rejoiced as it had not done since the end of the war celebrations. Australia, the formidable, unbeatable Australia, were hammered down—and by eight wickets too. Len Hutton, Denis Compton, Bill Edrich, our greatest and longest serving stars, had never been in a side that had beaten them in a series. When last an England captain had claimed the Ashes I was five, and here it was happening again before an English crowd that was no more phlegmatic than a Spanish mob at a bullfight.

My own contribution was dismally small, just four runs before departing to one of Lindwall's thunderbolt deliveries, but I do not recall anybody registering unusual disappointment or being hyper-critical. The milk of human kindness was in plentiful supply once England had won.

We started this epic match to the usual cannonade from Alec Bedser, this time supplemented by the fire of Freddie Trueman who came to the Australians as a new bowler with something of a 'wild man' reputation and stayed to impress them as a fast bowler of control and guile. Things were going smoothly enough Australia's way when, after an hour,

Arthur Morris turned his back on Bedser, gazed over Evans' head as he padded up, and to his consternation was given out l.b.w. as the ball whipped back. During the lunch break, rain slicked the top of the wicket and from that time onwards the Ashes started to come home.

Bedser and Trueman punched holes in the batting until only Lindwall and the tail-enders were left. So Ray hit every ball within driving distance and in no time Australia had climbed to the respectability of 275.

It was during his innings that I made my first contribution towards winning back the Ashes. I dropped him at deep extra-cover! He skied the ball and I stood still, intending to leave it for the man behind me to move forward and take. Suddenly I remembered it was Alec Bedser, tired from bowling and heavy of foot, so I turned and ran for the catch. I got underneath the ball just in time for it to pop out of my hands.

Before that first day ended I was witness, fortunately from a distance, of the most terrifying over I have ever seen bowled. Lindwall unleashed it at Hutton in the closing minutes and shocked the crowd. It was lightning fast and wickedly hostile. Two bumpers reared up at the England captain, the second hitting the handle of his bat, the ball seeming to hover in the air as the Australian fieldsmen came leaping forward from their Carmody-field placings. It dropped short of their stretching fingers and England breathed.

Subsequently England's innings was given a good start by Hutton, Edrich and the recalled Peter May, and the only time it threatened to founder was when Denis Compton and I were batting together. He and I have a reputation for being stroke makers. We belied it that day. Denis spent an hour for sixteen runs, but I was worse, getting only two in half that time. Our displays gave dour Trevor Bailey and jaunty Godfrey Evans the chance to end the series on a high note. This they accepted and England finished with the negligible lead of 31 on the first innings.

We knew all through the series that our strong suit on this Oval wicket would be the Surrey spinners Lock and

Laker, but when our first innings ended it seemed impossible that they could have enough runs to bowl, particularly as we had to bat fourth on a dry pitch.

Then came the revelation in the shape of the bowling of Lock, an indifferent performer at Leeds, but a magician on his own wicket. But before that came a battle of tactics between the two captains.

Before the start of the Australian innings Hassett ordered the heavy roller to be put on. This was a move more in the interests of his bowlers than his batsmen. The pitch had taken some spin for most of the match and if the dry surface was broken more it was fairly obvious that England's fourth innings task would be troublesome indeed.

Hutton countered this move by bringing his own spinners to the crease almost immediately. The pitch possessed nothing for the pace bowlers as Arthur Morris showed when he started off in a rush and thumped both Bedser and Trueman. It was a confident, challenging start, but after two overs Trueman retired to a close fielding position. Lock was on at the pavilion end and the Australian innings began to stutter.

Bedser was allowed one more over, then the old firm of Lock and Laker, spinning trouble incorporated, were established in business together. Laker started the collapse among these spin-shy Australians. There used to be a theory years ago that off-spin bowling was meat and drink to Australian batsmen, that they welcomed it with whoops of delight and fell over themselves hammering it to all parts of the globe. This may have been true of the pre-war Australian, which would explain the lack of Test opportunities of a bowler like Tom Goddard, but the more recent generations of Australians get in a most dreadful state of confusion at the sight of it.

In this innings, for instance, Hassett could have done nothing in his short innings to have established confidence among the rest of his batsmen watching from the balcony. Twice he was beaten by Laker in the Surrey bowler's first over, and to the last ball of the over performed a shuffling dance which landed him in front of his stumps in a comfortable position for an l.b.w. decision. Hassett, quite the best armed of the Australian batsmen, was not impressive. The reason, I believe, is that Australian wickets do not encourage the Laker type spin. Consequently, no matter how complete a batsman may be technically, he will always discover mysteries in bowling which is unusual to him.

The batting collapse which followed will supply me with fireside memories throughout my old age. Relentlessly I shall bore my grandchildren to tears with repeated descriptions of the fall of each wicket. I will have no mercy on them for never has there been such a day in English cricket.

In ninety minutes, half the Australians were gone. In one nerve wracking spell of fifteen minutes, four of them popped out of the pavilion, took guard and popped back again. The crowd cheered excitedly at the fall of each wicket, just as the Romans might have done when the lions made their entrance into the Colosseum. It was a most un-cricket like noise, but one I could well understand. I myself felt so excited that my hands trembled and I would willingly have made a roaring noise with the crowd just to relieve the tension inside me.

It seemed unbelievable. We were hammering them after all these years. In the middle Tony Lock and Freddie Trueman were falling into each other's arms as they hurled themselves about picking up close to the wicket catches. (Afterwards there was some criticism of these two for displaying their elation. It came from the stiff-upper-lip school who look at all success and failure in the same fashion as that celebrated war heroine Mrs. Miniver.)

Probably at the back of everyone's mind was the thought that the Australians might suddenly rise to the level of their great past and hit their way out of trouble. That jubilant stroke maker Neil Harvey would obviously be a big factor in any such plan. When the left-hander faced up to Lock, Hutton and his bowler pondered deeply as they adjusted the short-leg fieldsmen, tearing at Harvey's nerves before the ball was bowled. When at last it was delivered, it pitched outside the off-stump and Harvey, probably thinking of that packed leg-side field, considered it a gratuitous four runs through the sparse covering on the off. He went flat out for a drive, and his off-stump was jerked back.

Morris, Miller, Hole—at last the procession halted with as fine a display of bold hitting as one is likely to see in such a position in a Test match. It came in the main from Ron Archer, with ample support from Alan Davidson. These two all-rounders, although primarily bowlers, removed much of the menace from the bowling with an array of clean, powerful strokes. Their innings were bespattered with sixes and fours, and they not only prolonged the Australian innings to tea but began to put some bloom back on its cheeks. After the break England became defensive-minded and the last four wickets were whittled away without much more fuss.

Thus England were left to score 132 with time not a factor. For this happy position Lock must take the main credit. I do not suppose I have since seen him bowl as well as this for England. His control and spin were magnificent on a pitch that was far from being a bad one.

Yet while England needed runs the issue was always open, as was shown when Hutton, the batting inspiration of the side, the man savouring the greatest moment of his career, ran himself out. He tried to steal a doubtful second run to a shot fielded by Jimmy de Courcy, one of the star fielders in a side of star fielders. Hutton was prone to do extraordinary things like this every now and again. He could be batting like an angel when all of a sudden he would do something completely out of character, almost as if he blanked out momentarily.

But we reached our target, slowly and with the issue in doubt most of the way. The Australian failing was that they had nobody to use the wicket. Lindwall bowled masterly at medium pace and not until he pitched two bumpers which Bill Edrich, a fine hooker, promptly hit for four, did the tension ease.

In accordance with Test tradition Hassett and Morris bowled the closing overs. Denis Compton fittingly hit the winning run, and before the stumps could be pulled, the huge crowd swept across the playing area like the hordes of Gengis Khan—only much happier. Through it all the Surrey secretary Brian Castor, pleaded unavailingly over the loud speaker for them to keep clear of the table, while I stood on the balcony of the players' room, having done so little towards winning this game, with a lump in my throat. A few minutes later I washed it away with champagne.

Members of both teams held a great party after that match during which Hassett showed the unerring accuracy of all Australian fieldsmen by hitting the clock on the wall with a half-pint mug. I arrived home from the match, which had finished at three o'clock in the afternoon, at two thirty the following morning. I do not claim this as a record. I fancy some of the other players were even later!

The outstanding lesson of the tour from the Australian point of view, was that in England on the post-war Test pitches strong spin bowling was even more important than before. And that was Australia's weakest branch.

Yet in Keith Miller they possessed a fast bowler who never seemed to deteriorate. I sometimes think it was a shame Miller ever batted for he was very nearly the greatest quick bowler of all time, and had he not been saddled with the title 'all-rounder' I believe he would have achieved that distinction.

For all his reputation as a batsman, I was not greatly impressed by him. He always looked good when hitting the ball, but so untidy in defence. Somehow my over-riding impression of Miller playing defensive shots is of him constantly falling over himself. But maybe I am being unduly harsh.

Miller was a cricketer in the grand tradition. For him to take the new ball was no guarantee that he was going to bowl fast. He might run through the usual range of pace changes normal to a fast bowler, or he might come off that raking stride of his and bowl off-break, leg-break or googlie. He was unpredictable, unorthodox, the Bohemian of cricket. Yet whatever he did was seldom less than great and I know of no more disturbing prospect than standing up to Miller when the wicket was helpful and Australia were in trouble. Likewise, he would stand nonchalantly upright at slip, chin in hand, presumably wondering about the bet he had put on the three o'clock race. Yet put a chance anywhere near him and he snapped it up.

He enjoyed his cricket and liked everybody to join in, particularly the crowd. On an occasion at Taunton, he was bowling in a match that was steadily going to sleep, the crowd with it. So Miller promptly let go three bouncers in succession and the crowd woke up to cat-call him. That was much more to his liking.

Miller would share sweets with children on the boundary fence, throw the ball into the crowd, as he did after the Lord's Test of 1956, and so quite casually built himself into a legend. Miller was the great showman allied to the great cricketer, an unusual and exhilarating combination.

Altogether it was a good season for the professional captain, and in Gloucestershire Jack Crapp, the county's first paid leader since 1873, took us into joint sixth place in the championship, our highest since 1947. Had it not been for an abysmal spell in mid-summer when we failed to collect a single point from five matches we might have been an even greater power in the land.

Crapp, incidentally, demonstrated during the match with Sussex at Cheltenham that a professional could be as delicate in his handling of a situation as an amateur, and more so than some.

A topsy-turvy match in which Sussex had been forced to follow on was coming to its close with Gloucestershire going full out for victory during the extra half hour. Then David Sheppard suddenly instructed his bowlers to bowl leg theory to the usual packed on-side field, a move that always brings feeling in its wake. The crowd cat-called and slow handclapped and the Gloucestershire players felt irked that they should be robbed of victory by a method that was considered of doubtful pedigree in Test matches and outrageous in county games.

Eventually Jack Crapp walked out to the wicket and pointed

out to Sheppard that in the circumstances there was little point in playing the remaining fifteen minutes, that it was a waste of everyone's time. With that Sheppard immediately switched back to the attack, Ian Thomson took three wickets in four balls and Gloucestershire were thankful to escape with a draw as Andy Wilson played out the last over with number eleven at the other end.

Incidentally, I finished the season top of both the batting and the bowling averages for Gloucestershire, an honour which kept me happy right through the winter until we arrived in the West Indies. At that point my sense of humour began to take a battering.

CHAPTER TEN

CARIBBEAN CAULDRON

THE winter in the West Indies in 1953–54 was hot. By the time the M.C.C. had been there a little while it was positively torrid. I fancy that this tour might go down as the most unpleasant, the most controversial of all time, and I say that having both read and heard vivid descriptions of the 1932–33 bodyline tour of Australia.

As a goodwill mission the tour of the West Indies was a fiasco. It was punctuated by a riot, bad manners and actions on the part of some players which, to my mind, were tantamount to cheating.

In some quarters, and not all in the islands, there has been a great deal of effort expended in trying to shovel most of the responsibility for this tempestuous series on to the shoulders of the Englishmen. As one who was on that trip and on most occasions in a seat too close to the fire for comfort, I would refute this suggestion in the strongest possible terms. I make no attempt to whitewash either myself or my team mates. There were one or two incidents in which we were not seen at our best, but in legal terms I would enter a defence of 'extreme provocation'.

Seldom can any set of professional men, selected representatives of their country, have been asked to perform their jobs in more exasperating and unreal circumstances. The M.C.C. players deserve every credit for their behaviour in the West Indies, and in the few cases where there were lapses from the highest standard, I would point out that human nature being what it is, we might justifiably have reacted more vigorously.

That this trip proved a failure was not the fault of the

English players. Any man who says so speaks without true regard for the facts. In the West Indies the fabulous is an everyday occurrence. Their world is strange, exotic, violent, a bewildering place in which to dump a group of cricketers snatched from the greyness of England in December. This is the world of silver beaches and lilting calypsos, of rum and gambling, of politics and knife fights, of couples producing half a dozen children before they marry, claiming to be in the exalted state of 'living independently'. This then is the West Indies, not perhaps as a sociologist would see it, but as an England cricketer saw it.

But before we plunged into the Caribbean cauldron we stopped off at Bermuda for a whale of a time and three games which were of no importance and of little value from our point of view. Purely from a selfish outlook the matches did no more than allow us the chance to get used to the heat and take a little exercise. As regards batting practice, the matches were pointless for the ball bounced an unnatural height from the matting-on-concrete wickets. Still, it was a pleasant interlude during which Len Hutton and I played the Governor of the island and its top lawyer at golf.

So to Jamaica and the tour proper. Uneasiness was apparent from the moment we landed. To start with the atmosphere was too heavily charged for the liking of most of the English players. The ordinary people in the street looked upon this series as for the world championship, as we had just beaten Australia. And quite rightly they wanted to give us a thorough drubbing. At the other end of the social scale was a large faction which repeatedly buttonholed us at banquets and cocktail parties with the plea: "You must beat these chaps. Life here will be unbearable if you don't." To receive constant reminders couched in these phrases and others even more dramatic, can become a little trying.

In addition, we spent three weeks in Jamaica crowded into a hotel with several West Indian players, managing in our irritation at constantly falling over each other, to make the hackles rise on friend and foe alike.

With relief we got down to the job of playing serious cricket with two matches against Jamaica, an island which had never been beaten by the M.C.C. We promptly shattered them by an innings in the first match and drew the second. This was a happy start, particularly as Willie Watson and I slammed into the slow left-handers of Alf Valentine, just to disturb any optimism he might have about the forthcoming Tests.

The second match proved of considerable interest. George Headley, that master batsman of the 'thirties, had been brought back to Jamaica on a wave of sentiment, backed by £1,000 in subscriptions from the public. He had missed the first island match through being hit on the elbow during the M.C.C.'s loosening up fixture against Combined Parishes. Now he was in the side and it was completely obvious to everyone, including the West Indian selectors, that whether he did anything or nothing, Headley had to be in the side for the First Test. The West Indies Test sides always manage to find room for the local hero of the island on which they happen to be playing their match. Had Headley not been included, it was an open secret that the match would either be boycotted or there would be a riot. In view of what happened later, I am inclined to think that the rioters would have held sway.

As it was, Headley by revealing himself still a useful player if not a great one—he still had a taste for the hook, which our bowlers used to their own advantage—made the selectors' job reasonably easy by defending for four hours for half a century.

Less significant at the time was the fact that J. K. Holt was allowed to stay at the wicket after he had been quite patently caught when in his early twenties. I speak not on my own authority, because I was not playing in the match, but on that of just about all the M.C.C. players in the middle. There was never any suggestion that it was anything more than an umpiring error, yet Holt went on to complete 152 and play himself into the First Test.

The First Test was played at Sabina Park, the ground

ving off (*above*) and hitting out.

(*Above*) Tony Lock throws up his hands exultantly after clean bowling Neil Harvey, the Australian left-handed batsman. Final Test, Oval, 1953.

And (*below*) the same player about to run out Jimmy de Courcy, the Australian batsman, during the final Test at the Oval in 1953.

where M.C.C.'s quick bowlers had ruined Jamaica's record. On the basis of that game and with the wicket shiny and seemingly fast, Hutton dismissed all his spinners except Lock, and called up pace men Brian Statham, Freddie Trueman, Alan Moss and Trevor Bailey to carry the England attack. It was a gamble Hutton was to make again at a later date in Australia, and each time the result was disastrous. To our dismay the Sabina Park pitch possessed little pace and the West Indies made a good score.

The England first innings was about as reassuring as a fall down a lift shaft. Ramadhin and Valentine quickly showed us that what they did in England in 1950, they could do equally well in the bright light and on the easy wickets of the West Indies.

When our innings ended we began to get some real idea of the texture of a West Indian crowd when it was roused. Because Valentine was nursing a split finger and his quick bowlers were tired, Jeff Stollmeyer decided not to enforce the follow-on. Uproar greeted this news when it reached the crowd, and their equanimity was not improved when the England bowlers started to plough through the West Indian batting. Everton Weekes and 'Lucky' McWatt rescued the innings and England were presented with the far from impossible task on this pitch of making 457 to win.

By the end of the fifth day England had reached 227 for two and the crowd was making it apparent on every possible occasion that Stollmeyer's future was very uncertain. Before Stollmeyer made his bat-on decision, I was of the belief that the toughest skippering job in cricket must have been in captaining a weak England soon after the war. At Sabina Park I revised my opinion.

By the time England reached 277 for two the ground was a vat of unrest. Then the desperate Stollmeyer did just what Hutton had done in the first innings and switched to leg theory with Esmond Kentish bowling to a leg-side field of seven.

Just before lunch I was at the other end to Peter May when the future England captain shaped to play at a ball outside the leg stump, changed his mind and as the ball flicked his pads was given out caught behind the wicket. This decision was nothing less than terrible. At no time was May's bat within a foot of the ball.

At lunch-time a hundred extra police were drafted into the ground to keep Stollmeyer's critics at a distance in the event of England winning. At the airport airline officials carefully searched the plane in which he was to leave the island after the match.

As it happened, these precautions were unnecessary. In the circumstances England's batsmen turned out Stollmeyer's best friends and West Indies won comfortably.

But worse than the taste of defeat in our mouths was the broad hint we had received as to how we could expect the umpiring to be conducted in the tour.

In the first innings Holt was promising to make good in his first Test with a hundred. He was 6 runs off the target when umpire Perry Burke, a sound official, adjudged him l.b.w. to Statham. As reward for this decision Burke's wife, who was in the crowd, was punched in the face by a man (probably a gambler with money on Holt's hundred), and his father dropped in the docks. After that the umpiring deteriorated.

We Englishmen often complained about the umpiring, but perhaps my judgment would err sometimes if I were an umpire whose family was likely to be terrorised. I think I would rather be a popular umpire than go home to a wife who has been beaten by a mob!

The logical way round this problem is to bring umpires from outside the West Indies, possibly Australia, and say go hang the cost, and if that is impossible the M.C.C. should request that Barbadians umpire in Jamaica, Jamaicans in Barbados, and so on, so that there is never the possibility of a local man being victimised. But I imagine the main obstacle to suggestions of this sort would be the fierce local pride that burns throughout the islands.

Against Barbados in the match before the Second Test we won by one wicket, the final runs coming when Alan Moss, who found it difficult to contact the ball with his bat, placed his faith in his pads and collected three leg-byes.

Ken Suttle, the sprightly Sussex left-hander, scored well in each innings, yet was not included in the Test side. Instead a place was found for player-manager Charlie Palmer on the strength of his being an all-rounder, and while the West Indies were scoring nearly seven hundred runs in their two innings he was asked to bowl only 5 overs—one less than Denis Compton. It was an illogical piece of selection.

The first innings of the Barbados Test was rock bottom as far as England were concerned. From the moment that innings ended, we gradually improved as a side until, by the time the last two Tests arrived, we were a formidable unit.

We started the match well enough with the first three West Indians out for 25, and then Clyde Walcott dumped us on our backs with a double century. During this innings Walcott hit the ball harder than any other man I have played against in a Test. It almost seared the fast outfield, and what a contrast it provided to the English batting to follow.

We got stuck in one of the crawls that periodically mars our cricket. We stayed at the crease like a bunch of strokebound chumps while Ramadhin and Valentine wheeled down over after over on that perfect pitch and the crowd howled derision and demanded 'cricket'. My own contribution was 15 runs scraped together in over two hours, easily the worst innings I have ever played.

This nightmare effort started with my receiving two half volleys which I hit hard to mid-on. Whereupon Hutton came down the wicket and said: "Not too many shots. We'll play this one carefully." And we did, although careworn would be a better way to describe it.

Like all nightmares, my innings ended on an unforgettable note. Ramadhin bowled me a slow full toss outside the leg stump which I put straight back to him off the outside edge of the bat. Never shall I forget the effect that flaccid dismissal had on Hutton. He practically slumped over his bat, sheer disbelief and despair written in every line of his body. For over four hours he had defended, subduing all his own great strokes, in his determination to follow the plan he had set for England. I do not think it ever occurred to him that while the plan suited his own talents, it was alien to those of some members of his side.

As I walked dejectedly back to the pavilion, I left him at the wicket looking like a man betrayed. And when he started batting again, it was as if he had suddenly gone berserk. He raced down the wicket, hitting and swishing at everything, almost as though a note of hysteria had crept into his batting which, for so long before, had been dour and canny.

The happiest moment in the England dressing-room came when our first innings ended and we knew that never again could we play as badly. From that point onwards we began to look like world champions, even if it was too late to save the Second Test.

The West Indies set us 495 to win and we set about the job like a side jealous of its reputation. We played strokes this time, Hutton, May, Compton and myself, and although we went down to defeat I like to think that we produced batting in that fourth innings fit to stand with anything that the brilliant West Indians had produced.

The umpiring was good in this match, except for one deplorable decision, and again I was in a particularly good position to see as I was batting at the other end. This time Denis Compton was the victim within 7 runs of what would have been his first Test century since playing against the South Africans in 1951. As often happened when England were going well, Stollmeyer came on to bowl his mixture of leg-breaks and googlies. To Compton he pitched a googlie well outside the off-stump and the ball hit the batsman's pads as he reached across. Stollmeyer made a noise in his throat, not a proper appeal but the sound non-bowlers make when they beat a batsman who is going well. As much as anything it is an intimation to their sceptical colleagues in the field that they have performed a notable feat.

Well, Stollmeyer made this noise and Compton was given

out l.b.w. to a ball that could never possibly have hit the wicket. For some moments there was considerable embarrassment in the middle.

After the Barbados match we left for Georgetown knowing that we had to win the Third Test to give ourselves a chance. With three Tests left, there was still in front of us the jute matting of Port-of-Spain, a match which even the optimistic West Indians would not bet on being anything but a draw.

So in preparation for the grand assault we took on British Guiana, a poor side, and thrashed them, Willie Watson and I putting on over four hundred together. Incidentally, Hutton gave another example here of his tremendous shrewdness in assessing a match. When he came back to the pavilion he said to me: "You'll get a bucketful of runs here." Yet he himself had scored 0 and only been at the crease a few minutes.

I think one of the reasons for the feeling against the M.C.C. among some of the crowds was that we were too successful against the island sides. We treated them as no other touring side had treated them before, and their supporters did not like to see their heroes tumbled. Among these volatile people that dislike grew into a positive feeling, although I would say at once that the hospitality and friendliness away from the cricket grounds was overwhelming.

As we had determined, the Third Test provided us with our triumph. It also produced the Georgetown riot, which was not nearly so acceptable.

After winning the toss for the first time in eight Tests, Hutton manoeuvred our batting into an impressive position. This was one of his great Test innings, and I describe it thus realising all the implications. He batted for nearly eight hours, chancelessly, rigid in defence, perfect in stroke play. This was the great cricketer, the cool master of every situation that arose.

Hutton's batting was equalled in excellence only by Statham's bowling. On that shirt-front wicket he sent back Worrell, Stollmeyer and Walcott for 10 runs, bowling Stollmeyer with a ball that pitched on the leg-stump and hit the off.

It rained after that, and so interrupted the West Indian batting slide until the next day.

Their batting was dominated by Everton Weekes who deserved a hundred but just failed to reach it. He was bowled by Lock, and it is a strange thing that no matter what his bowling form may be against anyone else, the Surrey man invariably performs well against Weekes. With Weekes a good cutter and fierce hitter of the ball with almost any stroke, this is not easy to explain.

Yet explosion point came when McWatt and the inevitable Holt were making the West Indians' last ditch stand and doing it pretty well. They had reached 98 and were going for the second run to complete the century stand when Peter May's throw ran out McWatt by a couple of yards. There was no possible doubt about umpire Badge Menzies' decision, yet it still sparked off the Georgetown riot.

Whatever was behind this shameful and frightening outbreak of violence I shall never know. Rum, politics, gambling —all the theories were aired. All I know is that someone threw a bottle, and in the next second it was raining bottles and chunks of wood. Peter May came steaming into the middle, the first refugee from the boundary. We gathered in the centre of the wicket, fifteen fearful men in white in that cauldron of anger. Mounted police and the riot squad appeared. So did a West Indian official who suggested to Hutton that anything might happen and that he had better lead us off the field. The answer was pure Yorkshire: "We'll stay. We want a couple more wickets tonight."

So we stayed, And we did the right thing, for as tough as it was I shudder to think what might have happened had we made a move towards the pavilion with the riot at its height. Gradually the hubbub died down, the tension greatly eased by that wonderful clown Johnny Wardle who kept picking up the empty bottles, pretending to drink out of them and then staggering away 'pickled'. Wardle's humour was never more welcome.

But from our point of view the brightest moment in all that

trouble came when an uneasy peace had been restored and a boy went round the playing area clearing the bottles. Some joker in the crowd threw another at him, whereupon he started flinging them back as fast as he could pick them off the ground. He peppered that section of the crowd with bottles—with a lovely left-hand throw, too.

We got the wicket for which we risked our necks. When play restarted Ramadhin appeared at the wicket, but showed little interest in staying and we trooped off at the end of a hectic day, forming a bodyguard for umpire Menzies.

Poor Menzies went in fear of his life, for he was one of two new umpires introduced to the game after Hutton had objected to the original choice. The police cordoned his house for three or four days.

As a footnote to the match I would add that J. K. Holt was twice caught at the wicket by Godfrey Evans standing back to the quicker bowlers, and each time given not out. He went on to score 48 in the first innings and 64 in the second. The job of bowling to Mr. Holt was becoming rather trying.

The inevitable squall was not far away and it blew up in the Fourth Test on the Port-of-Spain matting with myself unfortunately playing the starring role. Denis Compton was given the ball for the last over before lunch on the first day and immediately hit a successful streak. Stollmeyer lofted a catch straight back to him. Weekes took a single to get off the mark, and there was Holt at the receiving end. Off the last ball of the morning session he tried a square drive to a googlie pitched wide of the off-stump, and edged the ball gently into my hands at slip.

I pocketed the ball gratefully and in the same movement started to walk to the pavilion for lunch. After a few paces I realised that I was alone, so a little uncertainly I looked over my shoulder to see that Holt was still at the wicket. I could hardly believe my eyes. I called to him: "Come on, then," but still he stayed. Hutton walked in from mid-off, disbelief etched on his face, calling to umpire Achong: "What about it,

Ellis?" Compton joined in the dialogue saying: "Give him out, Ellis."

Then Achong made his important contribution. He said: "No, not out."

For the first and, I hope the last time, I lost my temper on the cricket field. I flung the ball down, called to Holt: "That's the fourth bloody time," and stalked off to lunch to the hissing and booing of the crowd.

From this distance of time I suppose I was wrong, but as I have said before in this book, I believe that a batsman should walk when he knows he is out, and whether he be English, Australian, West Indian, South African or Pakistani, the rule holds good. And in the electric atmosphere in which these Tests were played I considered it morally wrong for a batsman to worsen the situation by this kind of thing.

As it was, by showing that I was made of flesh and blood and possessor of a temper, it was I who became the villain of the piece. Neither did my black deeds end with Holt.

Facing the bowling of Trevor Bailey, Everton Weekes attempted a square cut and hit the ball into Dick Spooner's gloves with the thickest under-edge you ever saw. More disbelief as umpire Woods gave him not out. This time Weekes turned to Spooner and said, "I'm sorry." Disconsolately wandering up the wicket at the end of the over, Spooner and I were speaking our minds on the subject, when Woods heard us and complained to Hutton.

The skipper said to us: "Cut down the talking." Afterwards the umpire explained that he had heard the sound of bat on ball, but had not seen the ball deviate from its line of flight.

Fortunately these aberrations in the umpiring had little effect on the match for it never shaped like a game of cricket. No match at Port-of-Spain has reached a definite decision since the matting pitch was laid down in 1934. The bowlers were there solely to feed the ball to the batsmen and the only hope they had was that a batsman would eventually become exhausted and get himself out. This did not happen often as the scores indicate.

The West Indies ran to 681, their highest score in Test cricket, before declaring and so putting themselves into a position from which they could hardly lose the series. When we topped the five hundred and avoided the follow-on, there was nothing left except some time to kill.

On this tour Freddie Trueman found himself labelled as the 'wild man' of the party, the sort of reputation it is almost impossible to shake off. Yet this Fourth Test produced the only incident I can recall in which the Yorkshireman was definitely at fault. He hit Ferguson, a far better leg-spinner than batsman, with a bumper and then walked back to the end of his run up and waited there, hands on hips, a lone figure of defiance.

The rest of us clustered round the likeable Ferguson, but Trueman seemed to think it a sign of weakness in a fast bowler to say sorry. Later he apologised after Hutton had spoken to him.

The Trueman of those days was a rough, tough lad who came from a hard background. He prickled with hostility and after his successes against India reckoned he had to bowl every batsman out. His natural belligerence on the cricket field would have meant nothing in a series against Australia, but in the West Indies, where the fast bowler is a controversial figure whatever his nature, he was greeted as blood brother to the Demon King.

Tony Lock was another who suffered because his tremendous keenness was mis-interpreted. The crowd took a dislike to him mainly because he shows quite openly that he wants a wicket with every ball. But is this such a bad thing?

The nerve-tearing belligerence of Lock and Trueman is half their power and it would be a foolish captain who discarded it by trying to discipline them into the calm, collected mould of say, a Peter May.

All in all, Trueman was nowhere near as bad as he was painted, and Lock was a first-class tourist. Yet it was almost impossible to avoid trouble on this trip as I had found out in

Barbados where I came close to being sent home because of an incident at a cocktail party.

It happened on a Saturday night and with Sunday a day-off we were relaxing, just as teams have relaxed ever since cricket was played on Broadha'penny Down with the Bat and Ball Inn nearby. It was just an ordinary party, as far from being a debauch as it was from being a Sunday-school outing, and it was attended by a myriad dignitaries from the islands.

One of these gentlemen—I had no idea who he was at the time—accosted me with the words: "I think the trouble with your English side is that the players do too much drinking."

I replied: "What business is it of yours? These are responsible Test cricketers who have never let their pleasure interfere with their cricket. They drink, but not to excess." I then enlarged upon the theme.

Apart from an occasional choking feeling, I thought no more about the incident until I was tipped off that an influential person had overheard the conversation and accused me of disrespect, that cables had started travelling to the M.C.C. in London, and that there was every possibility that I was going to be shipped home.

I was at my wits end. If I, as a professional, was sent home it would mean the end of my international career. Eventually the matter was sorted out by Len Hutton and Charlie Palmer with the aid of diplomacy. I breathed again and deduced that the moral from the incident was never to speak to strange men at parties.

That run-satiated Fourth Test saw the end of the series for Brian Statham, our prize asset among the fast bowlers. He strained himself and was not fit in time for the vital last match, the one we had to win to draw the rubber. Among other achievements Statham had proved the fallibility of Worrell.

But if there was no Statham at Sabina Park, there certainly was a Bailey. After Hutton had lost the toss, spirits in the England dressing room plummeted, yet just before tea we were joyfully padding up to take our turn to bat. That West Indian first innings just went crazy as Bailey took seven for 34 on a pitch slightly damp but still a good one to bat on. There is probably no bowler in the world as adept as Bailey at extracting maximum help from a pitch, and on this day he was altogether too much for the West Indians.

Thus the stage was set for another great Hutton innings. Everyone in the England team knew, I think, that he was going to get a hundred, but he fooled us all and got two hundred. Never have I seen a man so determined to win a match on his own if necessary. Nothing would turn him away from the victory he needed to sustain his record as a successful captain, and in his efforts he collected the only double century in a Test match by a touring captain of England. It was impossible to bowl at him with hope, and when his innings ended after nearly nine hours it was again because of one of these nagging, off-field incidents.

As Hutton walked off the field at tea-time, a man met him in front of the pavilion and said: "The Chief Minister would like to congratulate you." Hutton, who would play his major innings from the depths of a trance, obviously did not comprehend fully what was going on. He was exhausted, careworn and fully conscious that he had only a twenty-minute break before batting again. Vaguely he said "thank you" to Mr. Bustamente, held out a limp hand, turned and walked into the pavilion. The idea seemed to be that photographers should take pictures of Bustamente and Hutton together, but Hutton was not around.

By the time Hutton had taken off his gloves, the outcry had gone up from the aide that he had insulted the Chief Minister. People flashed in and out of the dressing-room, explanations were made and Hutton practically had to agree to an apology, which in the circumstances was just ridiculous.

From the turmoil of tea Hutton went back to the middle and was out almost immediately. So what was possibly the greatest captain's innings of all time ended in a welter of smashed concentration.

But Hutton had his consolation, for we won by nine wickets and the series was saved after that disastrous beginning.

So the tour of those lush, primitive islands drew to its close on a more peaceful note than seemed possible at one time.

Except off the field, of course, where even in the serenity of Sabina Park an argument broke out in the crowd and ended only when one man drew a revolver and cleared acres of ground around him as people bolted out of range.

Such is cricket in the West Indies.

CHAPTER ELEVEN

THE RISE OF TYSON

MODERN Test cricket is a non-stop merry-go-round of hard work and travel. By its very nature it overshadows the county programme and a regular England player will probably miss ten matches for his county each summer, and possibly more if he is rested before the Tests. In the winter he is whisked away to continue the same job in different conditions.

This period in my career was a particularly tough one. In 1953 Australia were the opposition, in 1953–54 the West Indies, in 1954 Pakistan and 1954–55 Australia again. It is hard to imagine a more exacting programme than that. Of all the series that against Pakistan in 1954 should have been the closest to a rest period, but through something akin to a freak result the rubber was drawn at one game each, Pakistan winning the last match at the Oval.

The first Test was a washout, the second was won by England by an innings and 129 runs, in the third rain saved the tourists from a pounding, and the fourth was won by Pakistan largely through England underestimating them. This is not to belittle a great bowling performance by Fazal Mahmood, yet it is true that England used the match as a trial horse for the Australian tour ahead. Tyson (then an unknown quantity), Loader, McConnon and Wardle were entrusted with the attack and were not impressive.

Secondly, the confidence of that effervescent character Godfrey Evans combined with our own estimation of the Pakistanis' worth, led us to the conclusion that we could win as we liked on the Monday evening of the match instead, as would normally have happened, leaving the result over until the following morning. So, from needing only 59 runs to win with seven wickets in hand, we tobogganed to defeat.

On that sobering note we sailed to engage the major enemy, Australia, on their own terrain. This trip is the ultimate ambition of every first-class cricketer and I earned my place more on the strength of my performances for Gloucestershire, for whom I scored heavily, than for my deeds against Pakistan.

So off we went, holding the Ashes, leaving behind a lot of people who believed we would not still have them when we returned in the Spring. The difference between the Australian and England teams in 1953 had been very slight, and although we had finished the series creditably in the West Indies since then, we had at the last moment hit this sour note against the juniors of the cricket world, Pakistan.

For me, this trip which had meant so much, turned out to be one long worry, and had it not been for a century in the Fifth Test it might well have brought to a summary end my chances in international cricket.

We knew before we left, in fact even the Australians must have known from the composition of the party, that we were going to hit them with a battery of fast bowlers. Fast bowling on overseas wickets has always been the lynch-pin in Hutton's tactics, yet the main question as we left Tilbury seemed to be who was going to do the fast bowling? Brian Statham was in the party, but his support in the genuine pace department would have to come from Peter Loader and Frank Tyson, both of whom were relatively new to Test cricket. Tyson had a reputation for being a bowler for three or four overs only, and although he had shown stamina in bowling against the Pakistan tail-enders he had certainly shown no signs of hustling Australian batsmen to defeat. Our future seemed to be very much in the lap of the gods.

And at Bunbury in a picnic match against a Western Australian Country XI it seemed that the gods were looking the other way. In that game, against minor opposition, Tyson never shaped like a fast bowler. He bowled in every direction except at the stumps and became the target for the wags in the crowd.

Yet in a few weeks this uncontrollable whirlwind had written his name large in the history of fast bowling as time and again he brought the cream of Australian Test batting to its knees. Tyson always bowled with the speed of fury, but not until he made various adjustments to run up and action did he suddenly become the fearsome prospect he was to remain throughout the series.

The change was as staggering as it was unexpected. Tyson went into the First Test, at Brisbane, when Hutton repeated the gamble of the West Indies and played all his fast bowlers. His figures of 1 for 160 in 29 overs speak for themselves and England were whipped by an innings and 154 runs. But from that match onwards Tyson began to extract full revenge for the hammering he had taken from the Australians that day.

Even so, it is doubtful if he would have enjoyed the triumph of the Second Test had he not bowled magnificently in the match prior to the Test, against Victoria. It was at Melbourne against the State team that he first realised his potential as he hurled out six batsmen in the first innings, including Neil Harvey whom he beat with eight deliveries.

That match marked the arrival of a new bowling star and the eclipse of a great one. Alec Bedser, the great man of English cricket since 1946, lost his Test place and so virtually came to the end of his international career. As with all these happenings, luck took a heavy hand in the proceedings.

Early in the tour Bedser had been struck down with shingles, an illness of tremendous weakening and lowering effect. He was not really fit for the First Test at Brisbane, yet because England needed him so badly he went into the match and was hammered with the rest of our attack. Had he declined to play, as he was quite entitled to do, he would have been an automatic choice for the Second Test and Tyson's chance of glory would have been postponed indefinitely.

I did not play at Brisbane as I was down with 'flu, but I came in for the Second Test in place of Denis Compton who was nursing a broken hand. We won the match, a glorious, fluctuating game, on the fast bowling of Statham and Tyson. An English pair had arrived to compare with Lindwall and Miller.

Arthur Morris skippered Australia, put England in on winning the toss, and then stood by while his bowlers put us out again. We looked booked for defeat. Our bowlers kept the Australian lead down to 74, but we knew from our experiences of 1953 that even this lead could be formidable. Indeed, Australia were in a happy position when they dismissed Hutton, Bailey and myself in the second innings. Then came the setback. Peter May produced a beautiful hundred, Colin Cowdrey a half century and the Australians found themselves needing 223, no great total, to win.

My contribution to the England second innings was 0. The ball was bowled by Bill Johnston and even as I drove and got an outside edge, I thought instinctively: 'You're out and you're in trouble.' Bill Bowes, England fast bowler turned journalist, thought along the same lines for he wrote that it was a performance that would mean a long climb back to international cricket for Graveney.

Another with the same idea was Hutton. After that he did not seem to care greatly whether I played or not, and in five months in Australia I played only fifteen first-class innings. My sole use to him after my Sydney effort was as a stand-in to rest his other batsmen.

From being potential winners at Sydney, the Australians were blasted into defeat as all except Harvey wilted before the Tyson onslaught. This was pace, the like of which they had not seen in the days when all the bowling fire had been on their side.

Hutton's handling of his fast bowlers in this innings and throughout the rest of the series was a revelation. He always made sure that they had stamina to spare for another effort, and if he made it a very slow game of cricket, he achieved his ambition and beat Australia.

Our next major engagement was the Third Test, and

not unexpectedly I was not included in the England side. The match followed a similar pattern to that at Sydney except that this time the thunder and lightning of the fast bowlers struck even harder.

England started batting secure in the knowledge that because of a strain Keith Miller would not bowl, and before you could believe your eyes he had appeared at the bowling crease and sent Hutton, Edrich and Compton back to the pavilion.

Looking back, this tour marked the beginning of the dominance of the amateur batsman in English cricket again. Colin Cowdrey, a newcomer to Test cricket, scored a century fit to rank with the greatest. It was just sheer perfection and it ended when a freak ball from Ian Johnson pitched well outside the off-stump, broke across his pads as he shuffled into position and hit the leg-stump. The major value of Cowdrey's innings was that it was played on a wicket on which the ball was always likely to do something erratic.

After that Australia took a first innings lead, England batted their way into the game with May leading the way, and then once again Australia set about the apparently comfortable task of winning. This time they needed 240 and at one period they were in the reassuring position of being 79 for two. That night, with the pitch wearing the highest and the lowest in the land warned Australia's batsmen to forget Tyson and Statham and beware the off-cutters of Bob Appleyard.

On the face of it the advice was sound. In practice the fast bowlers proved hard to ignore. In seventy-nine minutes the match was all over for the addition of a further 36 runs and Tyson had gathered six wickets for 16 runs. In the first half hour he took three wickets in twenty-one balls. It was a victory worthy of the Cecil B. de Mille epic treatment, and it meant that from being one Test down, England were now one up.

In the middle of this match there occurred an event which was peculiar, to say the least of it. On the Saturday night I went out and looked at the wicket and found quarter inch cracks which threatened to develop into fissures the size of cart ruts before the game was over. It looked a reasonable bet that the match would be completed with a couple of days to spare.

On the Sunday the temperature was 108 degrees, so hot it was hard to breathe, and when I came out of the sea I was dry before I reached my towel.

On the Monday we assembled at the ground not only to find the wicket perfect, with no cracks, but actually soft. Immediately there was an outcry, mainly from the Australian Press, and a demand for an investigation. The obvious inference was that the pitch had been watered and rolled by the groundsman who was in charge of his First Test wicket. He, of course, denied this and an inquiry by the Melbourne Cricket Club supported him. Officially the dampness was caused by sweating under the covers, but if that is the case Australia must have the sweatiest wickets in the world!

At Adelaide we won the series and kept the Ashes, but I did not see much of the match. I spent most of my time watching the Australian tennis championships. My dereliction of team spirit came about this way.

After Melbourne I had made up my mind to fight my way back into the Test side. Every morning I rose at six o'clock and went for training spells, running and doing exercises, until I was super fit. I felt my batting form returning too, even though I was never certain where in the order I would be batting next. Then, having keyed myself up for this effort, I felt terribly depressed when the England team was announced without my name. I cannot recall another moment in my life when I had ever felt so fed up. Cricket and I were not on the best of terms, so in my disappointment I looked for something to help me relax and found it in tennis.

But before I could savour it, I had to run the gauntlet of Australian gatemen, itself a terrifying experience. The M.C.C. players had been told by Harry Hopman that any time we wanted to see any tennis, just get in touch with him and he would look after us. Innocently Johnny Wardle and I wandered out of the cricket ground across to the tennis where we confidently asked to see Mr. Hopman. Now nobody on the gate objected to our seeing Mr. Hopman, it was just that they refused to give him a message that we were there. We hung around for a while but found that far from increasing our chances of getting in, we were only adding to our own frustration.

So back to the cricket ground we went, this time to be refused admission because we did not have our tickets with us. They were in the dressing-room. The gateman was adamant—no tickets, no admission, even though we were wearing M.C.C. blazers and white flannels. After some minutes of futile argument, Johnny jumped over the gate ready to do murder, and I believe the only thing that stopped him was the thought of the publicity such a deed would arouse. Eventually this fracas was sorted out at managerial level, but after that I decided that all gatemen in Australia were men to be avoided.

England won the series at Adelaide with a colossal helping of what the boxing fraternity would term 'kideroo'. It was the bluff of Melbourne extended into a gigantic confidence trick. There the Australians had been told to watch out for Appleyard, only to be pole-axed by Tyson. Here there seemed no alternative to Appleyard as the match winner, and Hutton actually encouraged the idea, yet in the final count who should tumble the Australians again but Tyson and Statham.

The Australian first innings on a perfect pitch followed the expected pattern with the batsmen scoring reasonably well, particularly the tail-enders, and the pace bowlers supplying most of the menace. England's first innings was something new in the series for it revealed the spinners as coming into their own. While England batted slowly and carefully, Ian Johnson threw his spinners against the batsmen with fair success.

Australia's second innings saw the trend continued and Hutton took the extreme step of breaking up his deadly fast bowling pair after only two overs, putting Appleyard on in place of Statham. The Yorkshireman promptly removed Morris, Burke and Harvey, and so overnight everyone considered quite properly that Appleyard was the menace of the hour. Everybody said so, only this time louder than they did at Melbourne, and nobody louder than Bill O'Reilly, the man most players who saw him count as the greatest bowler of modern times.

What all these logical forecasts failed to take into account was Hutton's faith in fast bowling. Having been scalded by fast bowling for years, Hutton had implicit faith in it. So that when these Australian batsmen appeared at the crease in the morning their minds full of the Appleyard bogy, they saw at the bowling crease not the stolid Yorkshireman, but far back in the distance the relaxed figure of Tyson, and at the other end his unholy twin Statham. These two catapulted themselves into action and over a sustained spell of ninety minutes took six wickets while 34 runs were being added. When the Australian innings ended leaving England to score 94, Appleyard had not taken another wicket although the conditions would probably have suited him as much as anybody.

England scored the runs for the loss of five wickets after that electric man Miller shocked us by removing Hutton, Edrich and Cowdrey as neatly as you please. It was he who kept our nerves taut until the end, although for once he disappointed me with an action that fell below his own tremendously high standard of sportsmanship.

It happened when Peter May walked, having been caught by Miller at cover. Miller fell taking the catch and dropped the ball, although that was not obvious to those in the middle. To myself and those near me, it was perfectly plain that the ball was on the ground. Compton, at the other end to May, also spotted it and shouted to his colleague, but the message was lost in the noise of the crowd.

Miller, who has signalled to so many batsmen when he has failed to make a catch, let May go, explaining afterwards that he thought he had held the ball long enough for it to count as a catch.

Incidentally, this whole series was played under the umpiring eye of Neil McInnes, quite the best umpire I have ever met anywhere. And all round, the umpiring on the tour was absolutely first class.

By the time we reached Sydney for the last Test of the series I was almost back in favour. At least I was among the twelve for the match, although there was no guarantee that I was going to play. Come to that, there was no guarantee that any of us were going to play, for New South Wales was practically awash with the worst floods in its history. Nothing happened until the fourth day when we took an early lunch with a view to starting at two o'clock. Ten minutes before we were due in the middle I still did not know whether I was playing, then Hutton came across and said: "Pad up, Tom. You'd better come in with me."

That was how I became an England opening batsman. I had played in the spot a few times before, but without really fancying the job. The man, I think, who first put me in line for the rôle was Sir Donald Bradman, in a newspaper article in 1953. He suggested that I was equipped to face the new ball. So England gave me a run there, and while I was on trial George Emmett asked me if I would like to open for Gloucestershire to gain experience, but I felt I could not accept a regular opening place with the county as this would have affected Martin Young, Arthur Milton or Emmett himself, themselves competing for the first two places.

Yet at Sydney the experiment got away to a golden start and produced a century which had lavish praise tumbling about me. That was my first hundred against Australia and almost exactly half the runs came in boundaries. It was one of those days when everything went right. Each time I stretched my left foot down that easy-paced strip the ball seemed to be there to drive. Did the fact that I played eighteen holes of golf the day before have anything to do with it, although nobody mentioned that at a time when I was succeeding?

When I was 85, Miller went round the wicket to bowl to me and I promptly hit him for three fours. Whereupon he opened that great, generous heart of his and practically presented me with the century. Without a fine leg, he bowled a ball wide down the on-side to me. I missed it. So he put another in the same spot and I hit it for four.

Having been confounded by pace all season, the Australian batting now found itself bemused by spin. Wardle bowled his 'funny stuff' out of the back of the hand superbly, so that one began to think in terms of the professional bowling in the school net. As far as the Australians were concerned he was unplayable and for the first time since 1938 they had to follow on, and even then came within uncomfortable distance of defeat. In one day they lost fourteen wickets, and the legend of Australian batting invincibility was buried, perhaps for ever.

There was no question now that England were world champions, and our next 'fight', with New Zealand, was very much of an anti-climax. I continued as an opening batsman, scoring two centuries outside the Tests.

We found the cricket standard in New Zealand only little higher than that of the good English club, as was instanced by the fact that they were shot out for 26 on a wicket far from bad. Their best players are Bert Sutcliffe and Jack Reid, both of whom would be better if they played in a higher class of cricket. Sutcliffe, in fact, is not as good as he was when he was in England in 1949 as their star batsman. They have a number of medium paced bowlers, of whom Tony McGibbon is the pick, yet none is outstanding.

These observations led me to the conclusion that the New Zealanders and five-day Test cricket just had nothing in common. Yet because of this uncomfortable thing called prestige they come here this summer to play us on the same terms as do Australia, South Africa and the West Indies. Presumably it would be considered a slight if it were suggested officially that they were not ready for five-day matches, yet would it be? Can one really expect them to produce world-shattering cricket sides with their resources?

In 1949 it can be argued, they were underdogs, yet they still drew the series. But against that is the fact that the matches were over three days, their batting, with such players as Donnelly, Sutcliffe and Hadlee, was solid, and the English bowling was not as fearsome as it is now. I doubt very much if they have the batsmen to stand up to the present English attack.

The unfortunate aspect of five-day Tests is that they now seem to be established for all class of opposition for all time. If we beat the New Zealanders in three days, they would be in a position to turn round and say: "So what? You beat the West Indies three times in three days in 1957." And that argument is unanswerable.

But whatever strength the New Zealanders may prove to be, you can expect them to face the full might of England at least until we are two Tests in front. I think the memory of that defeat by Pakistan is too recent for us to experiment with new players and take chances before the series is won. And our men will be keener than ever this summer. They all want to spend next winter in Australia.

CHAPTER TWELVE

AN UNEASY SERIES

THE South Africans are too keen to win. By the end of 1955 when I had played in all five Tests against them, I had come to the conclusion that in their ruthless desire to prove themselves world beaters the South Africans had forgotten that basically cricket was a game which one is meant to enjoy a little even in these pressurised days of five-day Test matches.

As a consequence the 1955 summer proved an uneasy one, as I believe did the series in South Africa in 1956–57. There is more to life than cricket and there is more to cricket than just winning, as pleasant as that may be. There was the smack of gamesmanship about some of their play, and once they were two games down in the series and staging that brave fight back, they approached every situation with such unyielding ferocity that I, for one, felt distinct relief as each game drew to an end.

Not all the South Africans were out of this dedicated robot mould. Yet some, like opening batsman Jackie McGlew who, I am sure, never had a thought other than cricket, became fanatical in their pursuit of the result. Keenness, in fact, overflowed into fanaticism. I have played against Australia in matches that were diamond hard, yet always they have been marked by an air of give and take and humour that revealed itself in incidents and asides on the field. Never have I known anything like the brooding air of nervousness that settled over the Test series of 1955.

But for all their faults the South Africans performed well. They are one of the few international sides that have grown to greatness almost entirely on the strength of their fielding.

It had confounded Australia before they came to us, and it came perilously close to toppling us as well. Not only did they take just about every chance ranging from slight to reasonable, but it seemed to me they made a habit of catching the virtually uncatchable. Their fielding was actually fiery and menacing and the ability of almost any one of their number to swoop over the grass like a seagull over water to snatch a catch, has established the reputation of at least one of their players, namely Hugh Tayfield.

To my mind Tayfield is not a great bowler. In fact, I believe he has been treated rather lightly by English batsmen, just as Ramadhin was spared (relatively speaking) until the summer of 1957. While the temperamental Tayfield may be a moaner, a man who wails about decisions, his lunch or the colour of the umpire's hair until he gets the nerves of everyone around him raw, he is still a master of field-placing. That is his strength—that ring of acrobatic fieldsmen with grasping hands. Every time they take one of their super catches, so the remaining batsmen sink farther into their shells and the Tayfield legend grows. One of these fine Test days a batsman is going to chance his luck against the South African, and succeed. Then the myth of Tayfield as the world's greatest off-spinner will be cut down to man-size.

With a large helping of luck, good on my side, not so good for other people, my record of not being omitted from a Test side in England since 1952 continued to the end of the season. Actually I was dropped for the last Test, having made o against the South Africans for Gloucestershire at Cheltenham on the day before the selectors met to name the team. On the day following their announcement I made 98 but, with my name not in the list, I seemed to have left the effort too late. A reprieve arrived when Colin Cowdrey and Frank Tyson had to stand down and Trevor Bailey and myself were included.

The First Test at Nottingham brought to the scene England's new captain, Peter May, although it was not known at that time that he was to fill the position permanently. Hutton, after his regular triumphs, had been named as captain for all five matches, yet the back illness that had troubled him for some time cut short his career. He made several efforts to get fit for the series with South Africa, and when he failed, he moved out of the international cricket arena, and a few months later out of the game altogether.

Yet when Peter May led us to an innings win at Nottingham we had no idea that Hutton had left our ranks.

To a large degree the match was easily forgettable, although there were one or two points of interest. Among them was the pairing for the first time in England, and the only time in the series as it turned out, of those destroyers of Australia, Tyson and Statham. England had put together a reasonable score when McGlew and Goddard faced up to them.

Tyson was the principal in our duet. He was the man who had gone to Australia the rawest novice and returned a hero.

Frank sensed the situation as much as anyone, and he decided on a special effort for the occasion. He bowled his first ball to the left-handed Trevor Goddard, and it almost screamed past the batsman. Goddard scarcely had time to move before the ball thumped into the hands of Godfrey Evans, standing back in the distance.

Goddard was thunderstruck. Never in his life had he caught a glimpse of anything as fast as that. Neither had I, and I had been with Tyson in Australia. From the crowd there literally came a gasp of amazement, yet most of the older people among those watching had been educated on the bowling of Larwood and Voce.

In the South African second innings Tyson produced one of his shattering spells and the match was all over with a day to spare.

Tyson did not play in the second Test at Lord's which was just as well for on that green wicket he would have filled up the casualty wards for miles around. As it was Statham got along very well without him, and a new fast bowling star emerged to claw at batsmen's nerves.

I had spent a good deal of time watching the South Africans in the nets and I could not make out how they could afford to omit Pete Heine from the Nottingham match. He was big, fast, hostile and could make the ball move either way. For some reason England were spared Heine at Trent Bridge, but we ran into him at Lord's, or rather he ran into us.

For some time now pleas have flowed from Lord's urging the preparation of faster wickets in the interests of more entertaining cricket. After batting in the first innings on this strip prepared on their own doorstep, I came to the conclusion that this kind of cricket could be entertaining only if you were watching from a distance or bowling fast on it. But batting on it on that first day produced much the same feeling, I should imagine, as being executed publicly.

I was still opening the innings at the time, and when May won the toss Kenyon and I went to the wicket. He took guard and up thundered Heine, all six feet four inches of him, for the first ball of the match. It was dug-in just about the length mark and it catapulted off that marsh green pitch straight at the head of the batsman. Kenyon ducked and four eyebrows went up—his and mine. 'This,' I thought, 'is going to be pleasant.'

Heine at least, enjoyed himself in his First Test. He took five wickets in the first innings and was the man responsible for tumbling England out for 133. He played throughout the rest of the series and, in my estimation, established himself among the four best fast bowlers I have ever played against. And not only is he a world-class bowler, but he is a great fielder too, either close to the wicket or away from it. The catch he took off a long hit from Johnny Wardle at Lord's was magnificent.

Yet for all Heine's brilliance this match belonged to Brian Statham. When South Africa needed only 183 to win he bowled England to victory. He bowled unchanged at top pace throughout the South African innings, and fortunately from our point he had a two-hour rest half-way through the last day when bad light stopped play. Even so, it was a tremendous fast bowling achievement allying stamina and control. Of the nine wickets that fell, seven went to him, two to Wardle, and

Freddie Trueman disposed of Jack Cheetham, chipping his elbow with a lifting ball.

Afterwards Statham told me: "I could not have gone off for a rest and come back again. I just had to keep it up or I was finished."

Cheetham did not have the happiest experience on this tour. The elbow injury put him out of the next two Tests, during which time his side pulled up to level terms after being two games down. He came back in time for the match to decide the rubber at the Oval, and South Africa lost that, so that all three defeats were suffered under his captaincy (not that I attach much importance to that).

The Lord's Test was full of that uneasiness which marked the series. There were one or two unexpected umpiring developments during which Laurie Gray, the former Middlesex fast bowler officiating at his First Test, was unsighted and walked across to consult Frank Chester at square leg. On the second occasion he was told by Chester, as autocratic as he was dependable: "Do your own job."

For much of this series the players were unhappy about the umpiring, yet the players themselves by their attitudes, made it a dreadully hard rubber to umpire. At Lord's two players, one a South African, one an Englishman, stayed at the wicket after they had been legitimately caught. Yet if batsmen are going to go out of their way to fool umpires they can hardly complain when they receive a harsh decision.

Perhaps I am soft adopting this attitude. The Australians, for instance, never walk away from the wicket. If they get away with a decision they treat the matter as a huge joke. Arthur Morris, their left-handed opening bat, tells a story against himself in this respect. He was playing against the Duke of Norfolk's XI in a Sunday match when he snicked the ball to the wicket-keeper. Says Morris: "I had already turned my back on the umpire and was gazing nonchalantly over square leg when I remembered that this was a charity match and not a five-day Test. So I walked off to the pavilion."

All the same, I think a lot of the feeling would disappear

from Test matches if everybody followed the example of Headley Keith at Lord's. He put a catch to me at slip off Statham when the second innings was balanced between victory and defeat and without consulting the umpire turned round and asked: "Did you catch it, Tom?" I nodded and he marched off without hesitation.

The Manchester Test will live in my memory as long as I live—unfortunately. South Africa won, I scored 0 and 1, missed three catches and kept wicket for the only time in my life. Altogether it was nerve racking.

Godfrey Evans damaged a finger in the South African first innings, although he kept wicket for most of it, and Peter May asked the inevitable question: "Who has kept wicket before?" A long silence until it became obvious that somebody was going to experience something new in their cricket life. It turned out to be me, probably on the principle that from first slip I had only to move one pace to my left to be in position. As I had been bouncing catches on the Old Trafford turf, I was fatalistic about the switch as, indeed, I needed to be with Tyson, Bedser (recalled for an injured Statham), Bailey and Lock in attack. Paul Winslow, at number eight for South Africa, added to the already slightly unreal air of the proceedings by smiting a fantastic century, just about the only innings of note he has achieved in first-class cricket. He reached his hundred with a hit off Lock that carried clear of the television cameras.

Yet the most staggering moment for me came when South Africa started their second innings chasing 145 to win. McGlew took guard from Tyson, then as the fast bowler delivered, just hared up the wicket without offering a stroke. I gathered the ball cleanly in a position nearer the sight-screen than the wicket, and threw down the stumps, only to find the batsmen comfortably home for a single. That was one bye against me, yet it is my great pride that I conceded only one more in the innings. Keeping wicket was about the best thing I did in the match, even though my little finger can now be bent at all angles like a piece of rubber.

The best batting came from Denis Compton and Roy McLean in this game. Compton has always had a liking for the bowling of the South Africans and he played beautifully here. McLean made his mark by pulling Tyson for three spectacular fours.

England went to Leeds without Don Kenyon. The man who could have solved our opening bat problem for years, had been discarded. Kenyon is an enigma. For Worcestershire he is one of the heaviest scorers in county cricket. He is a fine player, completely equipped for his job, but for all his poker-face I fancy that he suffers from nerves in Test matches. His failure was a tragedy both for himself and England.

Not only was Kenyon demobbed, but I began bouncing up and down the order again. Trevor Bailey and Frank Lowson were our new opening pair with myself at six. Suffice to say that as far as most of us were concerned it was a poor game, most of the worthwhile performances coming from the South Africans.

For the Fifth Test, the one which was to decide the series, the England selectors still permuted the opening bat position, this time Jack Ikin being recalled and Brian Close named as his partner. Close batted quite well, but Ikin was unlucky to get struck in the stomach and had to retire. In terms of cold figures the new partners were no more successful than the old. Players come and go round this opening bat spot so fast that it is difficult to recall their names, let alone their performances.

On a pitch similar to that which had figured in our defeat of Australia in 1953, Lock and Laker saw us home after May and myself had scored well together in our second innings.

Yet this series, which I am convinced was better to watch than to play in, was not decided without more umpiring controversy. At Leeds there had been the unusually high proportion of ten l.b.w. decisions and at the Oval there were three more appeals that caused some bitterness.

To deal with the most straightforward one first, let me say that I thought the l.b.w. decision given against Russell Endean in South Africa's second innings was correct. I even believe Endean was less incensed about it than were some of his colleagues watching from the balcony. Endean was given l.b.w. trying to sweep Jim Laker's off-spinner, but because of the cramped way he plays the stroke from directly in front of his stumps, the South African must be particularly prone to this sort of dismissal.

The other two l.b.w. decisions were of far more importance. They were both of the hair-line variety and because they went against South Africa, the side that had fought back gallantly from being two matches down, there was considerable feeling over them. Indeed, those two verdicts can be said to have won the series for England.

The first occurred when Peter May moved back to play Tayfield's off-spin, missed the ball and was rapped on the pads. To the disbelief of the South Africans the appeal was turned down and May went on to score 89 not out and so bolster the England total to reasonable proportions.

The second decision went against Roy McLean. This ferocious Springbok batsman was capable of swinging a game at any stage, but on this occasion he again attempted to leg sweep Laker far too early in his innings. He was struck on the front pad with his left foot far down the pitch, a stroke far different from that of Endean, yet he too was given out l.b.w.

Now I do not say these decisions were wrong, yet I do know that they were close enough to divide the opinions of the England team as to their validity. But if we had doubts, the South Africans had none. They were convinced that they had been the victims of umpiring errors, and none more so than McLean and bowler Tayfield.

Incidentally, England won the series when Heine skied a catch to me at long-on. I still have the ball at home.

The season finished on a personal note of satisfaction. I took 159 off the South Africans at the Scarborough Festival, in the course of which innings I was able to get into perspective the off-spin of Tayfield. I also scored a century against Yorkshire and came within three runs of another against the Gentlemen. It was a reassuring way to face the winter.

CHAPTER THIRTEEN

HUTTON—MASTER BATSMAN RETIRES

WITH the end of the uneasy series against South Africa an era had passed in English cricket. England's first professional captain stepped down and Peter May moved into his place.

Hutton went out of the game with a record unequalled. He was a great batsman and a great captain, and he had pulled England from the bottom of the cricketing class to the top and kept us there. He was a difficult man. I do not think I ever met anybody who understood him, and I doubt if he understood himself. He could be a charming companion one moment, although it was always difficult to know whether he was pulling your leg or being serious, and the next moment look through you as if you were a pane of glass. He did not deliberately cut people dead. He had simply transported his mind to another world where he was tackling a problem of his own.

He was not a man to offer advice, neither was he one to ask it. Occasionally he would approach Alec Bedser or Godfrey Evans on the field, but in the main he nursed his own problems, so that in the end the worry came close to breaking him.

He was a great cricketer, but I do not think he was very keen on me. He put up with me until I failed in the Test at Sydney, and then he finished with me. We were two entirely different characters and I do not think that Hutton could ever reconcile my more carefree approach to cricket with the game that he played.

He was a strict captain who forbade his team to laugh or

joke on the field or fraternise with the enemy. He would allow no slovenliness among his players and would bark with the authority of a sergeant major: "Take your hands out of your pockets," as he passed by.

He was a great captain because he recognised that there was more to leading a side than just settling the tactics of his own team. He studied the natures of his opponents as well as their technical weaknesses.

In Australia he would deliberately slow down the game when one of their younger players came to the wicket eager to get on with the game. When an older hand was at the crease, he would speed it up so that at a time when they wanted leisure he bustled them. He adapted to cricket the methods of the department of psychological warfare.

His theories were dominated by his worship of speed, a throw back to the days when Lindwall and Miller were giving him a harrowing time while he was trying to adjust his play to his shortened left arm. He had seen the effect of speed on other batsmen and suffered from it himself. I think that each time he ran into a problem he put himself in the place of the opposing batsman and asked! 'What would I not fancy now?' And nine times out of ten the answer came back: 'A quickie'.

He appreciated better than anybody else in my cricketing life the power of pace, yet occasionally it let him down as when he twice lost Tests—in the West Indies and Australia— through relying completely on fast bowlers.

When he had reached a decision about a player he followed it relentlessly. He was able to kid out such a mighty player as Clyde Walcott, operating on his own wickets, in this way.

When Walcott appeared he deliberately and calmly brought a player up to silly point. It was a challenge to Walcott's pride and the giant West Indian slammed the ball past the fieldsman, who visibly paled. Hutton made as if to move the man even closer. Again Walcott tried to shift him, and this time pulled the ball into his wicket off the under edge of the bat.

As a batsman he must have been one of the greats of all time, yet I felt that he seldom did himself justice. He was a player who made those around him look like pigmies when the challenge was great enough. As when he scored a century at Lord's in 1953 after the crowd had jeered him for dropping three catches in the Australian innings, or as when he made up his mind that the last Test against the West Indies in 1953–54 would be won and he scored a double century.

Hutton was equipped with strokes and defence as no other batsman of my time was equipped, yet he would let bowlers bowl at him. He would allow moderate performers, men he could have driven to despair in the course of two overs, to bowl half volleys to him for hours on end, and he would do no more than push the occasional single. Then suddenly he would unveil his real greatness and we who were watching or batting with him, would get a glimpse of what we were missing the rest of the time.

It happened even during that wonderful double century at Kingston. Denis Atkinson, the medium paced man, was weak with bowling to him. Hutton was in no trouble, yet he only pushed away three half volleys. The next ball Atkinson pitched on a perfect length and Hutton moved down the wicket and hit him back over his head for six. It was all so strange.

The real factor that kept Hutton in chains, was, I believe, the way he had carried the responsibility of the England innings for years. He and Denis Compton were our only players boasting the mantle of greatness, and Denis, the laughing boy of cricket, had to tackle his problems in his own adventurous way. In the circumstances Hutton accepted as his responsibility the task of giving substances to the innings, and in the end this outlook meant that defence dominated his play. When bowlers were putting the pressure on he automatically found the answer in defence, never in playing a few of those beautiful shots of his. He would follow three breath-taking strokes with an hour's defence.

He had got so used to carrying us on his own shoulders that he forgot how to relax at the wicket.

When he was batting Hutton was lost to this world. He would bury himself in concentration and stay there until finally he was out. During this time he knew nobody. During a long innings he would wander into the pavilion for say, a tea break, put down his bat, take off gloves and cap and then sit slumped, staring at the wall speaking to nobody. Somebody would loosen his pads, somebody else would push a cup of tea in front of him. Automatically he would lift the cup and drink the tea, still looking ahead unblinkingly, until the call went up: "Umpires are out, skipper", then he would collect his belongings and disappear again, never having spoken a word.

A school of opinion exists that maintains Hutton was weak against fast bowling. It is not a theory to which I subscribe. By the time I knew him in 1950, he was a magnificent player of fast bowling. The only weakness he possessed as far as I could see, was against the bouncer. He did not like the ball that reared up round his chin, but then I have yet to meet anyone who does. More to the point, he played it badly. He did not hook, but neither did he accept the other logical alternative of leaving the ball alone. Instead he would position himself behind the ball and try to play it with a dead-bat defensive shot, a method that allows too small a margin for error. Consequently he was in trouble a number of times pushing the bouncer towards the short leg fielders.

To my mind that was his only weakness against any type of attack. The people he really fancied were the slow left-handers, the men who bowled on to that beautiful cover drive of his, the shot that was completely his own. Never have I seen the stroke played the way Hutton played it, with his left foot flung so far down the pitch that he was almost touching the grass, the bat sweeping away from his body in a full arc. That was an exhilarating sight.

Remembering his shortened arm caused by a war-time injury, I can only wonder at what he must have been like before the war. I once stood in on a conversation between he and Denis Compton in which Denis reckoned his best period was

1947–48, while Hutton thought he reached his own peak in 1939. He must have been a fabulous player.

As an off the field captain, Hutton made a reasonable speech at functions, never forgetting to include a crack about his "old friends Lindwall and Miller". Hutton is never likely to forget those two.

But being as he was there were a number of people who had no liking for him, both among cricketers and administrators. It is hard to understand a man who is almost unfathomable. Jim Laker, the exiled Yorkshireman, has no love for him. Rumour says their bitterness springs from the time Hutton tried to persuade Laker away from Surrey back to Yorkshire, and was rebutted for his efforts.

I once had personal experience of the feeling between the two. Hutton, Laker, Statham and myself were having a drink together when Hutton suddenly asked me: "Would you like to go to Australia, Tom?" I, of course, answered "yes". Then Hutton turned to Statham and asked the question again. "Would you like to go to Australia, Brian?" After Statham had said how much, the conversation lagged into a long silence during which nothing was said to Laker. It was most embarrassing.

Like a good many of the greatest batsmen, Hutton could be a selfish player. It was not unknown for him to take a single off the first ball of an over on a bad wicket, or to keep the bowling and take a single off the last ball on a good one. A player who opened regularly with him for a while once told me: "I take a look at the wicket when we go in and I can tell just when he is going to call me. I can almost start running before he hits the ball. The trouble is that he is such a good player that it is always too good a single to be refused."

This then, was the strange character who captained England and brought the pride back to our Test cricket. It was hard to like him, but it was equally hard to deny him his place in the history of the game. Of all his conquests, his greatest happiness came from twice defeating Australia in the rubber. Somehow they always remained the 'old enemy', possibly because they played as hard as he did.

There stepped into Hutton's place at the helm, Peter May, a Southerner of completely contrasting background to the Yorkshireman. Hutton learned his cricket in a council school playground and among the local boys in the evening. May's cricket was produced by coaching in the nets at Charterhouse and Cambridge University.

Yet as captain's they came out of the same mould.

Both approach the game in the tough, cautious manner, building up their position before they strike in much the same way as Field Marshal Montgomery would amass superior forces before joining battle. It is the policy of success.

Peter May learned the job of captaincy under Stuart Surridge with Surrey, and Len Hutton with England. The dynamic, zestful Surridge seems to have given less to his protégé than did Hutton. Typical of the Hutton-May approach to Test cricket is their handling of Johnny Wardle, the Yorkshire slow left-hander. When allowed to, he can bowl his unorthodox googlies and chinamen well enough to nonplus any batsman in the world, but neither Hutton nor Peter May was exactly keen on the idea. They could remember too well the loose balls he threw up among the good ones.

When Peter May took over the leadership of the side he was, if anything, a stricter disciplinarian than Hutton. He had a great deal to live up to, and he was determined not to be found wanting. In the field he was something of a tiger, not hesitating to tick a man off if he thought he warranted it.

Now his discipline is still keen, though a little easier. In essence England have fielded the same side since 1953, and now we all know exactly how he will react and what he expects of us. Consequently, when playing for England now one is filled with a wonderful feeling of confidence and superiority. We seem to be so well on top of every situation, and there is a definite purpose about all our moves. At no time has this been more marked than during the series against the West Indies last summer when they seemed to be a side without a pattern once Ramadhin had failed.

When talking of Len Hutton and his effect on English cricket, it is only proper to speak of that other post-war English giant, Denis Compton. Here indeed, was a contrast.

Compton, light hearted, gay, was a law unto himself with a bat in his hand. He would sweep the ball outrageously off his stumps (always to fine leg, never square), dab the next delivery off his middle stump to third man, and between these shots push back his hair and talk to everyone within listening range.

With him cricket was essentially the same game whether it was played over five days or over a limited number of overs during an afternoon. His sole object was to enjoy the game, and in pursuit of that ideal he made sure that everybody else did. A Compton bat always sounded better than anybody else's, rather as if he were playing the game with a double bass.

The difference between him and Hutton was that Compton was not prepared to be tied down. It irked him. Laker, who bowled to both of them, once told me that it was possible to keep Hutton quiet, but it was impossible to subdue Compton.

He reached rock bottom in his career round about 1952 when he found runs harder to get than emeralds. He came back, limping on a knee that was a shocking mess to reclaim a Test place at a time when it seemed impossible that he should be playing, let alone batting for England. After that I consider it was one of the saddest sights of all time when he missed making a century against the Australians at the Oval in 1956 by a handful of runs. Every cricketer in the world, even the Australians, wished one on him.

Compton was always a credit to the game he played so generously. His batting was undiluted genius that had little connection with the recognised canons of the game. The aim of every boy in these islands should be to adopt his approach to the game, but Heaven help the boy who tries to copy his batting. He will have his wicket knocked over every ball.

Because Compton would permit no attack to restrict him, I rate him a greater batsman than Hutton. Only one man would I class above Denis—Clyde Walcott, a batsman who would rise up in his majesty and reduce a world class attack to rabble in the course of a few overs.

Such batting is regal. It provides cricket's greatest spectacle.

CHAPTER FOURTEEN

GOODWILL TOURS

In February 1956 I went to the West Indies on what was known popularly as 'Swanton's apology' tour. This label stuck in spite of all the objections to it by the organiser, Mr. E. W. Swanton, the cricket writer of the *Daily Telegraph*. The object of the trip was, I believe, to eliminate the unpleasant memories of the M.C.C. tour a couple of years earlier, although as the only player in the party who had been on that tour I felt strongly that there was nothing about which we had to apologise. But, at least, this trip created goodwill.

Colin Cowdrey and Frank Tyson were the only other Test men included in the party and between us we got through a great deal of work before we returned home. While the results were not important tremendous interest was aroused over the clash between their stars and Tyson. This was the first time they had felt the hot breath of his pace and they were gathering experience for future reference. Particularly did he and Walcott take an interest in each other.

In Barbados Tyson's pace bowled him out while Walcott was still going through the motions of his twirling back-lift. Yet while Walcott was beaten for pace, Conrad Hunte, an accomplished batsman whom I was surprised did not come to England, took two centuries off us. He was also a brilliant cover-point.

In the second match Walcott made his entrance and exit all in the space of one ball. This time yorked by Tyson. By the time Walcott re-appeared for the second innings, his side was in trouble. We had broken through and Tyson had retired from the bowling line for a rest. Walcott gathered a few runs and then Tyson came on with the new ball. This was the supreme challenge. The Walcott reputation was at stake.

The West Indian responded by hitting Tyson expresses three times through the covers and scoring a magnificent century. It is on the strength of such performances that I rate him the world's best batsman.

After our makeshift team had done well to beat Trinidad, a side seldom defeated on its perfect wicket—Tyson taking the last wicket with the fifth ball of the final over—we faced a full West Indian eleven. From the New Zealand trip and neighbouring islands, Sobers, Collie Smith, Ramadhin, Kanhai, Weekes and Walcott were flown in to meet us. It was very flattering—and devastating. We were a prep. school combination compared with this team.

But it was all good fun. Cowdrey, not the slimmest of cricketers, captained us in that match. Once as he chased the ball to the boundary, and he moves extremely lightly and quickly, one of the members of the crowd called out to me: "Hey mister, your captain, him sure like the kitchen."

At another point a duel developed between Tyson and Weekes. Twice the little West Indian skied hook shots into the air and afterwards he said: "He's a bit too quick to hook"— a great tribute to Tyson from the man who, at that time, was about the best hooker in the world.

But while Tyson and Weekes were testing each other I was holding another conversation with a spectator over the boundary boards.

He observed: "Weekes, a great player."

Me: "How do you get him out?" (This is always a good question because these knowledgeable West Indians often know the answer.)

Him: "Mistuh, you don't wanna aim at the stumps. You wanna aim here."

He pointed to the stomach.

On the way home the terrifying Tyson was hit for two successive sixes by a Bermuda batsman named Cheesey Hughes.

We decided that this was a record as no reputable fast bowler had ever before been treated thus by a gentleman bearing such a name.

We were assured that we were the most popular team ever to visit the islands, although I think we helped our cause by losing frequently, All the same there was still bitterness not far below the surface at the memory of the M.C.C. tour, and the newspapers were having a vitriolic time re-printing pieces from Hutton's book, which had just been published.

In one paper he was described as the most unpopular man in the West Indies, but I do not suppose that worried him.

My cricket life has been bespattered with these short jaunts overseas in the middle of winter, sometimes, as happened in 1956–57, because I had missed the boat carrying the big men to a Test tour. When I had hoped to be with England in South Africa, I found myself with the Duke of Norfolk in the West Indies and Bill Edrich in India.

I am no lover of English winters because of their damp and cold and I can think of no better place to spend the dark months than in the sun-drenched Caribbean. These private tours are tremendous fun. We went to Jamaica by boat, only fourteen passengers aboard. From the time we left home until we got back I cannot recall off-hand a night when we did not have a party. This was my third trip to the island and easily the most enjoyable. It is much more fun touring places you have been to before because then you have friends there. It is easy to slip into the routine.

The cricket was hectic and non-stop and Willie Watson, Don Smith, Roy Marshall and myself had only two days' rest on the whole tour. The games were enjoyable, probably because they were not vital. Twice we beat Jamaica, who included Valentine, Collie Smith, Gilchrist, Dewdney, Alexander, Rae and my old friend J. K. Holt, who still kept getting runs.

Once we needed nearly 350 runs to win and scored them for the loss of seven wickets. One of the features of the tour was that we never had a bad start to our innings. Don Smith, of

Sussex, and Roy Marshall always performed well together at a pace above even time. On this occasion they hammered the new ball with no more respect than if it had been two hundred runs old.

Montego Bay was full of interest. Lord Cobham played and batted well for a half century, and the local groundsman demonstrated his own method of drying a pitch. He poured petrol on to the turf, then set light to it. When the flame had died down a fellow came along filling in the cracks with his thumb. On this occasion his thumb became stuck in a hot crack and he danced up and down in the middle of the pitch, still bent over, howling and cursing. It was quite a sight.

Later the Duke of Norfolk introduced himself into our attack in an effort to take his first wicket. To be cold-blooded about it, I suppose his chances of dismissing anybody were never really very high. He bowled lobs so slow that it seemed sometimes they were going backwards, and their direction was unpredictable. Nevertheless he had an invaluable ally in Colin Ingleby-Mackenzie, the Hampshire player who was keeping wicket.

He began talking to the local batsman between deliveries, pointing out to him what an honour it would be to become the great Duke's first victim. After some time the batsman, a happy-go-lucky fellow, was tickled pink at the idea. He grinned agreement, nodded to Colin and hared off down the wicket to meet the next delivery. He missed it, the Duke hopped in the air as he saw his victim yards out of his ground, and Colin dropped the ball. So Colin started talking again about the honour of being dismissed by the Duke of Norfolk, and three balls later the batsman was off down the pitch again. This time the Duke got his wicket.

It was on this trip that we first knew that Valentine was going to have to struggle when he came to England in 1957. He bowled badly against us, still spinning the ball considerably but without having the control of length that was once his hallmark.

Three weeks before leaving for the West Indies with the

Duke of Norfolk's 1957 side, I had returned home from a short visit to Calcutta with a side raised by Geoffrey Howard for the silver jubilee of the cricket association of Bengal.

On the plane going out, skipper Bill Edrich rose from his seat and made a thirteen-word speech. He said: "There is only one way to play this fortnight's cricket—the Scarborough way." With that we settled back to enjoy a junket in which the cricket was as bright as the social life.

We arrived at Calcutta at three o'clock on the Saturday morning and on the Sunday morning started playing against a strong Indian representative side that included such players as Hazare, Armanath and Gupte. When I had left home in Gloucestershire on Boxing Day, it had just started to snow, and here I was a few days later preparing to play cricket with Indians in great heat. What an extraordinary game this is now, with air travel as an ever present magic carpet.

I played in the first innings of the match, and then went down with dysentery on New Year's night. Between thinking that my last hour had come—I did not go into hospital until next morning—I was furious at missing the celebrations.

In the second match, at Bombay, we gave the Indian side a terrific hiding, scoring heavily at round about eighty runs an hour in true Scarborough fashion. I hit a century in both innings.

While I was in India, Jim Parks was flown home from the England side in South Africa and Alan Oakman went down with back trouble, and the members of our party made bets that I would be flown out. But it was not to be. Peter May decided against asking for a replacement and I was left with the thought that I was still not forgiven for some 'crime' which had cost me my place to South Africa originally.

From India I came back with the opinion that Gupte is the best leg-spin bowler in the world today, better even than Bruce Dooland. He is the only man of his type I have seen drop the ball on a length immediately. He has a beautiful action and bowls the googlie at least two different ways, possibly three. He could be a great threat when the Indians come here in 1959 for his is a type of bowling against which English batsmen get little practice.

The Australians evidently intend putting a lot of faith on the bowling of Dooland, now returned home to South Australia from Nottinghamshire, when we go out there in the winter, yet I feel anything Dooland can do Gupte can do better.

One of the saddest features of our cricket is the absence of leg-spin. It is the type of bowling most likely to dismiss a batsman on a good wicket, yet because its effectiveness is tinged with extravagance it is regarded with suspicion in English county cricket. Few captains are prepared to gamble runs off the loose ball against wickets off the good one.

Personally I, and I think most other batsmen, regard it as the most interesting type of bowling, a fact reflected in the number of us who try to bowl it on our occasional spells with the ball. Len Hutton, Jack Ikin, Colin Cowdrey, Ken Barrington and a dozen others (including myself) fancy ourselves as leg-spinners even if our skippers are more sceptical.

Some students of the game even go as far as to suggest that a batsman will always try to bowl the type of ball he himself considers most dangerous. On the basis of that argument it would seem that the case for a return to leg-spin is overwhelming.

CHAPTER FIFTEEN

DROPPED FROM TESTS

THE wet and dismal summer of 1956 had brought about the downfall of Tom Graveney, plus that of the Australians. The two matters were not unconnected.

The way the season started, there was no indication that I was going to end it lost in the wilderness, abandoned by selectors, and generally wondering where I was heading for next. By 1956 I had ironed out all my batting problems, so that I could hit the ball more or less where I wanted to, distributing my shots on either side of the wicket impartially. As a consequence, when I was in form I batted better than at any other time in my career. And I was in form for most of the season, my only really bad spell coming in June.

I was called to Lord's for the usual Test preliminary of playing for the M.C.C. against the Australians and scored runs reasonably well without being at my best. So to Nottingham for the First Test of the series where I was feeling happy enough until I holed out to first slip trying to drive the off-spin of Ian Johnson.

Incidentally, I am convinced that England could have lost that match instead of it being left drawn. We declared hoping that a wet wicket would aid the spinners. Instead it aided nobody, and was beautifully easy paced for batting. If the Australian batsmen had possessed more self-confidence they could have scored those runs, but as with so many visiting sides, the sight of water frightened them. They became so timid that even I was brought on to bowl.

This Australian party was picked, I should imagine, with

a view to countering the pace that had made England supreme on their wickets. Consequently they were of the solid, cautious type who found that they were at a disadvantage against the turning ball. Nevertheless, at Trent Bridge they had their chance for there was nothing in the wicket for either pace or spin.

In this match England solved one half of the opening batsman problem. Peter Richardson, the left-hander from Worcestershire, revealed himself as the man for the job, yet he was so close to being another failure. But for the tremendously quick thinking of Cowdrey and the negligence of Miller in failing to catch a return to the wicket, he must have been run out for five in the most scintillating merry-go-round I have seen in the middle of a Test wicket. In the second innings he escaped being caught by Burge off Lindwall for 0, and since then has established himself as England's Test opener.

The Lord's Test of 1956 will belong to Keith Miller for all time. His was a great bowling performance. Umpire Frank Lee described it as probably the greatest piece of sustained fast bowling he had ever seen. In its way it was a typical example of Miller at work. He had a pitch on which he could use the ball off the seam, and he was eager to get at us.

Any batsman who has ever faced Miller in this mood will never forget the experience. His whole person exudes belligerence. He waits impatiently at the bowling crease for the ball to be returned to him, calling and snapping his fingers, then off he goes to some unpredictable mark tossing back his mane of hair, his stride seemingly longer than ever. This is the Miller who can chivvy a batsman's nerves and force him into indiscretion.

Miller finished the match with ten wickets, having bowled 70 overs—and that at thirty-six years of age. I figured twice in his bag, and these failures cost me my Test place for the first time in this country since 1952.

Miller, ever willing to make life hard for a batsman, played on my liking for the cover drive in my second innings.

He suddenly switched to bowling round the wicket. let go a half volley wide of the off-stump and I touched a catch to Gil Langley as I chased it to drive. My effort, however unwilling, helped Langley establish a Test wicket-keeping record by dismissing nine men in a match.

This thought was no consolation as I made my way through the Long Room. I had failed and I could feel the cold shivers rippling up and down my spine. To fail at Lord's seems to be a personal matter, and the sight of those silent, illustrious members looking the other way as you pass through their ranks leaves no doubt as to their feelings in the matter.

Not far behind the Miller-Langley combination in deadliness in this match, was the savagery of Richie Benaud. Benaud with the bat is a hitter of fluctuating success. On this occasion he reached his peak and flayed the bowling of Trueman, Statham and Bailey. He raced to 97 and then was out attempting yet another big hit to bring his century. But was he so unlucky? By the reckoning of the England side he was caught out behind the wicket off his glove a few minutes after the start of his innings. Nevertheless, having been let off, he certainly stayed to stir the blood.

In stark, stumbling contrast was the innings of Ken Mackay at the other end. His was a performance that was as desperate to watch as it was useful to his side.

As an example of international batting, Mackay's display was easy to scoff at, yet the fact is the bowlers could not get him out. He is a deceptively difficult man to bowl to for he can let the ball pass closer to his stumps without playing than any other man I know.

Keith Miller says: "On a good track he is the hardest man I have ever bowled to." I would like to add the postscript that on one that turns he is the worst.

Soon after they had trampled on England, the Australians trampled even harder on Gloucestershire. Jack Wilson, the chubby slow left-hander who otherwise had an unsuccessful tour, routed us on a bad wicket at Bristol. But that game

(*Above*) Len Hutton and Alec Bedser lead out England at the Oval, with author and Peter May in rear of group.

(*Below*) Gloucestershire team group taken in 1948. (Standing, left to right) Neale, Cranfield, the author, Scott, Lambert, Cook, Wilson, B. S. Bloodworth (scorer). (Seated) Crapp, Goddard, B. O. Allen (captain), Barnett, Emmett.

(*Above*) Members of the M.C.C. team in Jamaica during 1953–54 tour.

(*Below*) Trevor Bailey, leaning against bar, with Denis Compton just in front of him, relaxing at a party in the West Indies.

brought us to the end of June and the termination of my bad spell. In the next match I hit 190 off Leicestershire and regained the golden touch of earlier in the summer.

But by then it was too late. My Test failures had caught up with me and I was omitted from the Third Test which England won to draw level in the series. Alan Oakman, the Sussex player, took my place, although the man who caused rejoicing among the selectors was Cyril Washbrook, himself a selector, brought back to Test cricket after being discarded nearly six years before. Washbrook not only succeeded, but he saved England.

Meanwhile runs continued to flow from my bat. I took a hundred off Middlesex and only narrowly missed one against Surrey. It is always good to take runs off the 'resident' champions, and this innings pleased me particularly because it involved a tough fight.

This sort of form, I reckoned, must surely put me back into the Test running. And it did. I was selected for the Fourth Test at Manchester, but did not play because of a hand injury and from then on I dropped out of the selectors' considerations in such a way that I can only guess I had been thought guilty of some misdemeanour.

The trouble started when Gloucestershire were playing Lancashire in the match before the Test. Twice before that game I had been hit on the knuckle of the right hand, and now it became jarred playing against the pace of my great companion-in-arms, Brian Statham. At the end of my second innings, the hand was painful and I immediately reported the matter to Cyril Washbrook, as a selector. He arranged for me to see a specialist in Manchester on the Wednesday afternoon, and on the Tuesday evening, after the Lancashire game, I flew home as I had been away for some time.

The next day I was back in Manchester when the England side began to assemble. I went to see the specialist and after a number of X-rays he told me: "I do not think you are in any shape to play."

Dejected (after all I had fought to get my Test place back),

I took the report to 'Gubby' Allen, the chairman of the selection committee. He agreed that I was not fit and Oakman was brought up for the match again.

At the team dinner that night Oakman, who had failed at Leeds, jocularly called to me: "You have probably cost me a trip to South Africa by not playing in this match."

I laughed and gagged back: "Why do you think I am not playing?"

In the light of later events these words, spoken by both of us in jest, took on an added significance.

While Jim Laker was re-writing Test history by taking nineteen Australian wickets at Manchester, I was resting from cricket. At the beginning of August I started playing again and took runs off Warwickshire. Just before the side for the Fifth Test was named I scored 200 against Glamorgan.

The hand was sound, the eye perfect. Yet not only was I not included in the England team for the Oval match, but my name was not among those for the South African tour the following winter.

Logically, I could not follow the pattern of events. Oakman had been dropped from the side, yet I, who had been good enough to be selected for the Fourth Test, was not brought back. Between the two matches my form, if anything, had improved. And I wanted to play.

My last chance to go to South Africa was to fill one of the last three vacancies. When I was not included in the party I came to the reluctant and puzzling conclusion that I had done something wrong.

What it was I had no idea, and even now I still have not. Other people, though, were not so short on theories.

One of the more ingenious expounded was that when I dropped out of the England team on the Wednesday, Peter May had come up to me and said: "Bad luck, Tom." Whereupon he shook my hand firmly and when I did not wince, May had concluded that I was 'swinging the lead'. That handgrip, allegedly, had squeezed me out of the South African trip.

Even in Gloucestershire it was being mooted that I was fit.

According to that theory, I was playing safe, refusing to risk any more failures against Australia, so that I could make sure of going on the winter tour.

Some of the edge was taken off this story by a Bristol doctor who, being a keen Gloucestershire supporter, was desperately keen on my playing for the county as we were in the middle of a fairly successful run. He examined my hand on the Friday (the second day of the Manchester Test) and said: "Unfortunately you cannot play for a week."

Afterwards, when the rumours were at their ripest and most hurtful, he wrote at length in the Bristol *Evening Post*, saying that it was quite impossible for me to play with my hand in its present state.

My omission from the M.C.C. side to tour South Africa brought a burst of indignation from Charlie Barnett, which he committed to paper and sent to the *Daily Telegraph*. Barnett himself was dropped from the England side in 1938 after three Test matches in which he had an average of 43, including 126 at Nottingham where he scored 99 before lunch, an innings that is still talked about. Neither was he selected for the South African tour that followed.

Wrote Barnett: "What evidence is there to show that the selectors are in favour of bright and attractive cricket? None at all. But there is plenty to show that they disapprove of anyone who takes a risk.

"Harold Gimblett received even shorter recognition for his efforts, but the worst crime against an attractive player must be this year's effort in sacking Tom Graveney, not so much from the Test match, but from the touring side to South Africa.

"It is little use wailing about unattractive cricket and falling gates if the hardest-hitting, highest run-making batsman in the country has his income from cricket slashed by fifty per cent because he failed in two Test matches against Australia."

Ironically, eleven years after he was dropped by England for South Africa, Barnett was made an honorary member of the M.C.C.

So I was left with a winter of perplexity, relieved by two short trips to India and the West Indies.

In my time I had been given plenty of chances, but that is no consolation for a man gazing moodily out of the window at the falling rain while the radio prepares to dispense the scores from South Africa.

CHAPTER SIXTEEN

ECLIPSE OF WEST INDIES

SLOWLY the winter passed. The West Indians arrived to the accompaniment of predictions that their batting would prove too much for our bowling and their bowling too much for our batting. These forecasts were not without some basis in fact.

The three Ws, as they have come to be known, formed the most formidable batting machine in the world. References to their bowling meant Ramadhin and nobody else, yet he had made such a habit of confounding England that there seemed no reason why he should not do it again. This, apparently, was to be the crucial season for an England side which though good, was still looked at with some doubt by the more exacting of the critics. What few people foresaw was that England would arise from this series wearing the mantle of greatness while West Indian cricket collapsed in a cloud of doubt and defeatism.

Before the series began I was told over a drink by a gleeful prospective mourner for English cricket: "These West Indians play because they enjoy playing. This season they will show up the English cricketers with their Civil Servant minds."

Unfortunately I never saw him again after that.

In the Graveney book of memoirs the 1957 season will have a special place all decorated with gold and silver and anything else that would mark it as outstanding. On a day on which the sun shone and the world looked green and wonderful, the team for the first Test was announced with my name among the twelve. Such a selection could mean only one thing—whatever my sin, I had done full penance. I was back in favour again, an England player. All I had to do now was to justify this belief with the bat.

But at Edgbaston I was not an England player. I was the man left out, not that this worried me a great deal for I knew now that I was in the running.

I stayed at Birmingham for the first day of the match and saw the last of Ramadhin as the scourge of England. He took seven wickets, including six for ten in one spell, and altogether looked a pretty formidable factor considering this was the first game of a series.

Next day I was released to play for Gloucestershire, for whom I scored a century against Warwickshire on the Saturday. So I missed the last chapter in the Ramadhin tale of success, which was a pity for I had suffered at his hands as much as anybody for a long time. Peter May and Colin Cowdrey killed the Ramadhin legend on the outskirts of smoky Birmingham as surely as if the little man had retired from Test cricket.

When England were faced with defeat, May scored 285 not out and Cowdrey 154 in a stand of 411. It was the biggest partnership ever made for England, but more important it shot to pieces the pre-conceived West Indian strategy for the whole tour. On the first day when England had been tumbling out, I felt that this was just one of those days when everything went wrong. I felt convinced that Ramadhin was made of flesh and blood, just like the rest of us. This stand proved it.

When Ramadhin was mastered during the last two days of that match, I gathered from the other England players later that the West Indian captain, John Goddard, seemed to be fumbling for a plan of action. For instance, when May and Cowdrey came together on the last morning of their stand together, he allowed them the luxury of playing themselves in against a defensive field.

I played in the last four Tests and this lack of policy was obvious then. It was as if Goddard had seen his ace trumped and was at a loss as what to do next.

166

England drew the Edgbaston match, but from then on the series was in perspective.

I came back to Test cricket at Lord's where England won by an innings and to which my contribution was o l.b.w. bowled Gilchrist. Believe me, when you are l.b.w. to Gilchrist, a man who is frighteningly fast and erratic, the quickest in the world at the moment I should think, you remember it for some time.

This was the match in which the West Indies reached low water mark. Never before in Test cricket have I seen any side sink so far.

To start with, their selection and tactics did not inspire confidence. The Lord's wicket was so green that without stumps and white lines it would have been impossible to tell the pitch from the outfield. In the face of these conditions West Indies preferred the fading and unpredictable spin of Valentine to the medium pace and batting of Atkinson. It was an incomprehensible decision.

As always in helpful conditions, Trevor Bailey was at his peak and in the match he harvested eleven wickets. Yet I cannot help thinking that Atkinson might have done nearly as good a job in the 'seam-up' Keith Miller style.

In fact, it was a wicket which the fast bowlers did not use as well as the fast-medium men, and I fancy Derek Shackleton of Hampshire, or Alec Bedser would have bowled out the world's best on this strip.

In these conditions, which were close to being dangerous, Colin Cowdrey hit another century while the demoralised West Indians dropped in round figures, ten catches. Everton Weekes, handicapped by sinus trouble throughout the series, provided a classic 90. Many people reckon this was the best innings played throughout the rubber. I would not argue with them.

I went to Nottingham for the Third Test with the uncomfortable knowledge that if I failed again I would be sent so far into the wilderness that it would need a safari to bring me back.

Within a few minutes of Peter May winning the toss I was face to face with my international future. Don Smith went quickly and I was on my way to the middle. It is an old and comforting thought now that I scored 258, batted something like eight hours, and went very well too, if you have no objection to my saying so.

Yet it was so nearly not so. The second ball I received ducked in late at me as I shaped to drive and carried about two yards wide of Garry Sobers at leg-slip. It was the sort of thing a lithe fielder like Sobers might have caught. He did not and I was saved.

After that everything was fine on that beautiful batting wicket. Peter Richardson who was himself engaged in scoring a hundred at the other end, wandered down the wicket occasionally to give encouragement. "O.K. now, son," he would say, or after a good over: "You're in for the day."

During that innings I got on terms with myself. I put aside the doubts that had assailed me during the few moments I was waiting to bat and played cricket just the way I liked to play cricket.

At lunch I was 47. Then Valentine bowled me a long hop that brought up my 50. By mid-afternoon my hundred had arrived, and during the applause Peter May stood on the England balcony, bent forward and tapped his head. I was to get my head down and play on.

My second century was completed with a straight drive off Gilchrist which brought joy to my heart. Periodically through my long stands with Richardson and May, Ramadhin appeared in the bowling line, was thumped hard and then replaced.

This was my first three figure score for England since Sydney in 1955, and throughout it first Richardson and then May kept up a stream of encouragement. Eventually I came to the conclusion that the only way I could get out on this wicket was by falling asleep, and soon afterwards was promptly bowled by Collie Smith, an off-spinner most sadly under-estimated by his skipper.

From then on the match went to a draw with Frank Worrell playing a most beautiful innings for 191 not out. On what I had seen in the West Indies, Worrell was the player among the three Ws I least expected to handle the new generation of English fast bowlers operating in our own conditions. Yet he went in first and played them magnificently. Surprisingly Worrell emerged from this tour as the most successful of the three.

Collie Smith too, passed a hundred and fifty in this match, a feat he was to achieve again later in the series, and he gave every sign of becoming a first-class performer once he shakes off some of his impetuosity.

Any signs of a West Indies batting revival was shattered at Leeds and England won a low scoring match by an innings. Peter Loader claimed the hat-trick and by so doing once again raised the question of how long such a fine bowler who both moves the ball and varies his pace, can be kept in reserve. The truth is that England are now in the happy state where they can pick any two of four or five quick bowlers and still have a good attack. For all Loader's feats some of the West Indian shots in their second innings when we did not bowl particularly well were scarcely credible. They looked then like a side with no more stomach for the fight.

And so it proved as England romped away to win by an innings and 237 runs at the Oval where the West Indies were dismissed for 89 and 86, the lowest scores in their Test history. It hardly seemed possible that this was the ending of a tour that had started on such a high note of confidence with such a braying of trumpets.

As at Nottingham, Peter Richardson and I both scored centuries. I find the Worcestershire player a wonderful partner. His judgment of a run is almost uncanny.

When the series was over there still remained one large black question mark. What went wrong with this West Indian side of all the talents? With Weekes, Worrell, Walcott and Ramadhin in the side it was impossible to deny their strength, yet in the final reckoning they were beaten with almost insolent ease by an England side which for three Tests was scarcely extended.

They came here with the reputation of being gay batsmen, each and every one of them capable of demoralising an attack in the course of a few overs. By the time they left it was obvious that when a side possesses a combination of world-class bowlers, as England do, no batsman is able to play all the strokes in the book and get away with it, no matter how sunny his nature. Great bowling is quite capable of subduing great batsmen.

But above the failure of individuals, was the failure of the side. They were a team which, from first to last were out-captained. In contrast to Peter May's approach to the game, the leadership of John Goddard seemed to lack purpose.

In 1950 Goddard had been able to toss the ball to Rama-dhin and Valentine and the job was done. This time Valentine was a spent force and Ramadhin was revealed as a human being and not a wizard. The result was that Goddard was suddenly faced with large problems, and he appeared to have no plan on which to fall back. It looked sometimes as if his policy had become caught up in the whirlwind of England supremacy and was flying here, there and everywhere.

An example of this tendency occurred in the Lord's Test where, having hopelessly misjudged the nature of this green wicket, he preferred Valentine to Atkinson and then bowled the slow left-hander for only three overs in the match. The selection and use of Valentine seemed a hopeless contra-diction.

Yet all in all Goddard was a captain deserving of sympathy. Apart from Worrell his big guns failed. Weekes and Walcott, the men the record books showed were probably the heaviest run makers in the world, were a disappointment to themselves, their skipper and the crowds who remembered their great deeds of the past.

For Weekes there was an excuse. Throughout the series he was plagued by sinus trouble and double vision, a tragedy in any circumstances but particularly so in the case of a player of the stamp of Weekes.

The failure of Walcott was not so easy to understand. Against the M.C.C. at Lord's he was regal as ever, yet once he had been injured at Birmingham in the First Test he became a fumbling giant. Almost invariably he fell to the off-spin of Jim Laker who brought his number of successes over Walcott to seven, generally tempting him to try to square cut. Quipped Laker: "It's lucky for me this fellow Walcott's playing."

I could not reconcile this Walcott with the man I rate as the world's greatest batsman. I could not believe that this was the man I had once seen lash the England bowling for a double century, starting his attack in the first over. This man who looked anything but a master, had once hit the most ferocious maiden over I have ever seen. Six times he slammed the ball and each time it went straight to an unfortunate fieldsman who would have been happy to have got out of the way. Trevor Bailey added a maiden to his bowling analysis, but it so easily might have yielded 24 runs.

Confidently I had tipped Walcott to score more runs than any other batsman on either side. And here he was the batting flop of the tour.

Why he should fall away like this I cannot explain. Probably Walcott cannot himself properly, for if batsmen knew what was preventing them getting runs they would soon remedy it. All I know is that when the heart went out of the West Indies and they looked a rabble, it was seldom any use their looking to Walcott for inspiration.

Dressing-room chatter around the county grounds suggested that there was feeling between he and Goddard over the captaincy of the side, though Walcott has denied it. Others contended Goddard should never have been brought out of semi-retirement for the job and that it should have gone to Walcott in the first place.

Whatever the reason for Walcott's poor showing, he stepped down off his pedestal as the West Indies number one hero and gave way to Frank Worrell, the player I and many other judges had reckoned would find life difficult against the fast bowlers.

With the batting machine wrecked, the West Indies were really in a pretty hopeless position once Ramadhin was conquered. Right away I should like to make it clear that I had played against Ramadhin several times in the past and there was scarcely any deterioration in his bowling in 1957. His eclipse was entirely due to the fact that for the first time in his life he was 'found out' by the English batsmen.

Still not all of us could read his mysterious hand action, but after the morale-boosting stand between May and Cowdrey at Edgbaston we tackled him with much more authority and confidence. Correspondingly Ramadhin's authority and confidence waned, and once that happened we were on top. He probably reached the lowest point of his illustrious career when he bowled ineffectively on a turning pitch at the Oval in conditions in which Tony Lock was making the ball 'talk'.

Yet in this same match he could still show a flash of genius. He still bowled Colin Cowdrey with his leg-break when the batsman was looking for the off-break. David Sheppard played Ramadhin's spin, I suspect, on his water-tight batting technique so that even if his reading of the break was incorrect he still survived.

Peter Richardson, who almost invariably played a long innings against the West Indies even if gathering only a small number of runs, was familiar with all Ramadhin's tricks, and I imagine that by the end of the tour I was, too. In any case, when the light was good I would watch which way the ball was spinning as it came through the air towards me, so that I was doubly armed.

After a couple of Tests Ramadhin knew that we had his measure and he lost some of his keenness to bowl. And that, as it turned out, was almost the end of the West Indies as an attacking force.

To add to their troubles not only was their batting (which

seemed impregnable with an accomplished player like Rohan Kanhai coming in at number seven) shattered, but for the first time in many series the English batsmen struck form together. Between us we hit eight centuries, while on the perfect batting wickets of the West Indies we had managed only six.

But whatever their immediate failings, the West Indians proved themselves of fine potential. Their young men were all good players, although I believe that Garfield Sobers, left-hand bat and left-arm bowler, will turn out the best of the lot. He played extremely well against Lock and Laker at the Oval and his only weakness is that occasionally he lets his head come back as he hits hopefully at the ball. Against England's bowling that generally meant the loss of his wicket.

Strangely, in this series both sides faced the same problem. That of finding a pair of opening batsmen. Having experimented successfully with Worrell, the West Indies have now retired to their own sunny islands to sort out their problem.

Meanwhile we appear to be no nearer deciding who will go in with Peter Richardson to start our innings. Our trouble would be over if David Sheppard were available regularly, and when his Church duties leave him free it is still in our interests to play him. On the other hand we are never likely to solve our problem while he is popping in and out of the team.

But the first essential in selecting an England opener is to pick a man who wants to do the job. Over the years we have experimented with Willie Watson, Colin Cowdrey and myself all people who were never very keen on opening an innings.

My personal choice for the job would be my county colleague Arthur Milton. It was a pity he broke a hand last season, for I feel he might well have been given a chance against the West Indies. Obviously he has been on the fringe of an England place for some years and he is certainly fully equipped to go into partnership with Richardson now. Sometimes as I watch him I think he does not realise how much talent he possesses. If he did he would not let bowlers subdue him when he could so easily handle them.

I seem to have made much this same criticism of Len Hutton—and he was not a bad opening bat!

CHAPTER SEVENTEEN

FACT AND FICTION

My career has stretched over the period in which English cricket rose from the depths, shook itself and then climbed to a greatness it may never have reached before. During that time I played with, or against the world's greatest players, learned to marvel at their strengths and be tolerant of their weaknesses, knowing that we were all undergoing the same incredible strain that is imposed upon us by five-day Test matches.

I have enjoyed success and put up with failure, although as so often seems to be the case the failures leave a more lasting impression in some people's minds than the successes. Why I should have failed, I have no idea.

Yet everybody else seemed to know ... I was frightened of Test matches, temperamentally unsound, preferred playing for Gloucestershire to playing for England, lacked concentration, and all in all possessed enough faults in my frame and brain to prevent me reaching the first eleven at school, let alone be considered by an experienced selection committee for a place in an international side.

As much as I hate disappointing the sensationalists, I must emphasise that I enjoy playing for England. A Test place to me is a sign that a man has reached the top of his profession, and I like the feeling as much as any business magnate in the City. In any case, to meet the best players in the world cannot help but add zest to the game.

Neither do I think I lack concentration at the wicket. I believe that as I settle into an innings so my reactions, my movements and my concentration, all click into gear automatically.

In short, I sail sublimely into a Test match feeling only little more tension than I do in an ordinary county match. And this in itself may be the cause of my downfall. Test matches do not usually produce as many bad balls as the county games and it may be that sometimes I try to make runs too fast. But always I have tried to play cricket on the basis that the ball is there to be struck hard on every possible occasion. It may bring some uncertainty into my play, but it gives me a great deal of enjoyment, too.

As the parade of stars has passed through my story, so I have paid tribute to them. Many of them were great players, some are verging on greatness now and will reach their peak in the near future.

Such a man is Peter May, who produced as the 1957 season was closing, an innings of extraordinary power. As he whipped the West Indian bowling for a century during the Scarborough Festival he played every shot known to man, apart from the sweep. Once, against Asgarali bowling medium-pace, he leaned on to his back foot and hit the ball straight over the bowler's head for six. I have only seen two other men, Clyde Walcott and Collie Smith, perform that shot.

To the public May is a slim young man. His build belies his power and stamina, and if he stays in the game long enough there will be a tinkling of smashed batting records such as has not been heard since the golden days of Bradman.

Away from the international glamour is a man who was a giant among giants—Alec Bedser. The remarkable thing about his bowling feats is that they were performed almost single-handed. Unlike most of the great bowlers of the game, Bedser was not one half of an illustrious pair. Lindwall and Miller, Gregory and Macdonald, Ramadhin and Valentine . . . the names trip off the tongue. In Australia on our last trip there was a parody going the rounds:

> "Ashes to ash and dust to dust,
> If Statham don't get you, Tyson must."

Getting some wicket-keeping tips from Godfrey Evans after the
Kent stumper had broken a finger in the Third Test against
South Africa, 1955.

Gloucestershire's greatest name, W. G. Grace.

Yet Alec, the big fellow, could claim that his achievements were all his own work, or nearly so. The strength of bowling pairs is that a batsman is never safe at either end. With Bedser that was not the case. No matter how good the bowler at the other end, he was never of the same calibre as the Surrey man. There was always a chance of escape, but in the end Bedser got them. He harried them and hunted them, using the conditions as few other bowlers have been able to do, pushing through a leg-cutter on soft wickets that came off like a Doug Wright leg-spinner, and in the end all the great ones were put into his bag.

Perhaps Bedser had no great bowling ally at the other end, but he had an ally infinitely more dangerous in Godfrey Evans. People argue about the greatest wicket-keeper there has ever been, but I have never heard anyone who has played with Evans say they saw anyone better. On any wicket, placid, unpredictable, or just downright wicked, he would stand up to the stumps to take Bedser's bounce and swing and break. And all the time he was like an extra short-leg fielder or slip, picking up acrobatic catches that left the victim dumbfounded. So he is a showman and occasionally he does drop the easy catch trying to make it look more spectacular than it is, but is that important? Genius must have a let-out somewhere.

Apart from being such a wonderful wicket-keeper, he is the prop on which the side's morale can always rest. Return the ball two yards wide of the stumps and he will scuttle across and take it so cleanly that it looks like a good throw. When spirits are beginning to flag at the end of a day under a tropical sun, Evans is still as chirpy as he was when he emerged from the pavilion first thing in the morning. His rallying cry as we come up to the last half hour—"It's the last session, gentlemen. They can't stop the clock going round"—puts heart into us all.

As a Test player Evans has reached the veteran stage, yet I am half convinced that he is getting better instead of deteriorating. He is a player who adds untold strength to the bowling power of a side, but none benefited more from his assistance than Bedser.

It might not be too fanciful to couple the names Bedser and Evans with the great bowling combinations of the game.

Of all the spinning pairs Lock and Laker are incomparable in this country. While Laker relies on length and flight as reinforcements to his spin, Lock pushes the ball through so fast that if it moves off the pitch he is almost impossible to play.

But overseas Lock loses much of his threat. On perfect batting wickets I would prefer the unorthodox wrist spin of Johnny Wardle.

Lock, too, is always likely to run into trouble over his action when abroad. His arm is far from being straight and a no-ball decision against him is always a possibility. It happened in the West Indies where he had to abandon his faster ball—and it was wickedly fast—because the umpires considered that to achieve such pace off so short a run he had to throw the ball.

Not that Lock is unique in possessing a suspect bowling action, and most of the other players have managed to survive scrutiny by international umpires. In that West Indies series Ramadhin became fed up with the way things were going and he let go two successive fast deliveries. One was a genuine bouncer and the other a beamer, a full-toss bowled straight at the head. Both were thrown, but neither brought reprimand from the umpire.

Cuan McCarthy, the South African fast bowler, delivered the ball with a bent wrist, and Ian Johnson was the greatest thrower in my experience. As he did not throw particularly accurately during the 1956 Tests, it was of no vital importance.

It would seem that there is an uneasy truce in cricket at present on this question of bowling actions, but I doubt if that is a unique situation in the history of the game.

One of the problem jobs over the years has been that of finding all-rounders for the top classes of the game. Before England began their winning run in 1952, there were various demands for bowlers 'who bat a bit' to bolster our suspect batting. But until Trevor Bailey emerged as the genuine article, the all-rounder spot remained a controversial one. In our desperation it was not easy for members of the public to see that a man who rates as an all-rounder in county cricket is far from being a Test class performer.

Specialists dominate the first-class game and unless a man is in the Miller-Mankad-Bailey mould it is scarcely worth his while trying to attempt the dual rôle in Test cricket. Australia neglected this principle in 1953 when they arrived here with too many all-rounders. Ron Archer and Alan Davidson were both better bowlers than batsmen and with Lindwall and Miller already there to open the bowling, there was not enough batting to carry the side.

The most recent example of a man who might be a great all-rounder were it not for five-day Tests is Frank Worrell. He might have been a wonderful bowler—his action is perfect—had he not been such a batsman.

It is a strange thing that since I have been playing cricket, Yorkshire have not figured among the county championship winners. They have always been a good side, one to earn respect, yet most of their post-war reputation has been based on the memories of greatness left by their formidable sides of the 'Thirties.

The Yorkshire players have no liking for being the underdogs to Surrey; the Yorkshire followers are attracted to the idea even less.

These Yorkshire people are hard taskmasters when they crowd into a cricket ground. Because they are hyper-critical they are either the best or the worst in the world to play before. They are full of pride and remember too well the days when there was not a county in the country which could live with them. In their blunt Northern natures, they still look upon Brian Sellers, tough, uncompromising, one of the great disciplinarians of the game, as the ideal captain and cricketer.

It is this constant living in the past that has made them such a hard crowd. They have rigid, unbending standards, and heaven help anyone who falls below them.

As a consequence the people who suffer most are their own players. The Yorkshire public's treatment of their own players falls a long way below the ideal. To allow the county captain, Billy Sutcliffe, to walk to the wicket in silence as happened in a match at Sheffield is little short of criminal. Sutcliffe, with Watson, both of whom have now left the county side, were two of the greatest hearted cricketers, yet because the Yorkshire team did not live up to a preconceived standard of their ability, Sutcliffe the captain was pilloried. Even on grounds where he could claim to be popular, his reception was luke-warm.

The fact that he was leading a fledgling side, heavy with players learning their jobs was of no account. Neither was it reckoned important that Sutcliffe had little say in the selection of his sides. To make a man skipper and then delegate half his power to the committee room is not, to my way of thinking, the ideal method for winning matches.

Because Sutcliffe suffered from an overdose of misplaced, carping criticism, so did the rest of the side. Youngsters who who were being introduced to the first-class game to ensure Yorkshire's cricketing future were made to wriggle under the microscope.

It is the easiest thing in the world to sit at the side during a match and criticise a player, perhaps scoff at him, maybe write him off. Cricket is far easier from sixty yards distance than it is in the middle.

When you first start it is a hard game. I found that and I was on my own as a new boy. It must be twice as tough when you are one of the four of five youngsters all striving to make the grade. They have to accept a responsibility such as I was protected from by the senior members of the Gloucestershire side.

Then, more than ever, consideration and tolerance is needed from their judges. Yorkshiremen too often forget that cricket is a game that originated in the South for the enjoyment of all. It was not meant to be conducted on the lines of trench-warfare.

Yorkshire now have the makings of a tremendous side, one which in two or three years time could be as dominant in the county game as Surrey are now. Pickles, Taylor, Stott,

Illingworth and others are all fine players in the making. As Taylor and Stott gather experience so their batting will reveal even greater richness than it does now, and the thought of Pickles, a genuinely fast bowler with a nose-diving follow-through, operating at the other end to Trueman is a terrifying one. This opening attack will reap destruction up and down the country for years to come.

The future of Yorkshire cricket is bright. Perhaps almost as bright as its past.

The Oval crowd, too, is partisan, but not with malicious intent. The South Londoners have feasted too well on success these recent years. They are impatient at anything or anyone that threatens to hold up the stream of Surrey victories, and as the sun rises over the ground the judge and jury, stationed over by the small scorebox (which also happens to be close to the bar) start to voice their opinions. These are very much to the point and are directed at both batsmen and bowlers. Their own men can get scalded as much as anyone else, for the Oval crowd is reluctant to admit the merit of defensive play, even though that art requires the greatest ability on their turning wickets.

But there is nothing deep-rooted about their criticism, even though they are a trifle too quick to use the slow hand-clap, a most insidious form of barracking. This handclap business is a disease that spreads quickly among a crowd. Its very anonymity makes it easier to commit. Better by far the man who fills his lungs and bawls across the ground: "Why don't you go 'ome, Graveney?" It may not be very original, but at least it demands some sort of courage or individuality.

Much of this slow-handclapping business is started by restless schoolboys, although to the player with the din in his ears this is no consolation. Boys get restless with a full day's cricket. Unless the sixes and fours are flying they take to wrestling and tumbling among themselves, and once they have tired themselves out the slow handclap is not far behind. It is significant that since the 'riot' during the M.C.C. tour, the Georgetown authorities in the West Indies have done away with the special

ey had for young spectators. Boys need to be among
g influence of adults, otherwise in their thoughtless-
can poison the atmosphere of a game with their
ing barracking.

In the main the English barracker lacks the wit or resource
of his Australian counterpart. 'Down under' their comments
can drop large chunks of humour into the tension of a match.
During our last tour there Neil Harvey, the Australian left-
hander, played and missed, played and missed, right through
the course of an over from Frank Tyson. Then came the shout
of the barracker: "Tyson, bowl him a piano and see if he can
play that."

Undoubtedly the best crowd to play in front of is at Lord's.
There they are cosmopolitan, very often not so interested in
the result as in basking in the cricket and enjoying the atmosphere of the ground. Cricket at headquarters has a charm and
grace all its own. Somehow the nervousness and bustle of the
1950's has been strained out of it. Every cricketer says there is
nothing like playing at Lord's. And they are all right, every
one of them.

Much of the public's attitude towards cricket is conditioned
by what they see and hear on television and read in the newspapers. This comprehensive coverage has taken the public by
the hand and led them, not always carefully, through the technical intricacies of the game and deep into the personal lives of
the players.

As a result England probably possesses the most knowledgeable cricket following the game has ever known in this
country. Cricket, mainly through television over the past few
years, has become a family sport, yet this new interest has cut
both ways.

With the televising of Test matches, there has tended to be
a drop in county attendance. In short, a national rather than a
local interest has been created. It is easy to call anything that
keeps people away from the grounds a bad thing, although in
this case I am not so sure. Surely anything that creates the
interest in cricket that modern television has done is for the

good of the game? If the television authorities were to report that, as well as the grounds being empty, nobody was watching their transmissions of the Test game, then that, surely, would be the time to become panic stricken.

More personal, from the player's point of view, is the attention paid him by the Press, attention which is not always the most tactful. In the main they do a good job for the game, but few players get by without an occasional clash with a journalist. Too often the interest of player and reporter are at variance. Both have their vastly different tasks to fulfil.

In my time I suppose I have shouldered as much criticism as most cricketers. In time of failure it has been heaped upon me by the cartload, and sometimes too, in moments of success the praise has been tinged with an ah-but-you-wait-till-next-time note.

Most cricketers adopt a defensive technique to newspaper criticism. Some refuse to read the papers in the mornings in case it upsets their concentration on the day's play ahead. They read their morning papers in the evening, so that another day's play acts as a buffer between them and the criticisms.

Others, like Len Hutton, adopted fireproof philosophies. Once, after he had been the victim of a most flamboyant attack in a widely-read newspaper, Hutton said calmly: "So they kick me to death on Monday. By Friday they will be calling me the best fellow on this earth. They've got to earn a living, same as anyone else, and it all evens out in the end."

My own reaction is to read the reports of my batting *only* when I have done well. My maxim is that I know better than anyone else when I have played badly and there is no need for me to be told about it.

As with every other profession, journalism has unreliable members in its ranks, gentlemen who dream up statements allegedly made by players. Fortunately, the players get to know them and so either avoid them or make sure any statements are non-committal.

Twice during the 1957 series against the West Indies I figured reluctantly in two news stories.

The first time occurred when I was dropped for the First Test at Birmingham. According to the story that appeared I was terribly upset at the way I had been omitted from the twelve. I had been playing in the nets when Brian Statham came out and told me: "Hard luck, son." After that I was supposed to have returned to the dressing-room where Peter May avoided me and everybody else was markedly unsympathetic.

This tale of woe could do a player in my position, trying to make my way back into the England side, no good. Neither did it. A few days later I received a letter from the Board of Control asking for an explanation.

I was named again for the Second Test and this produced yet another interview. On the Sunday the side was selected I was rung up at home and asked: "How do you feel about Ramadhin?"

I knew enough about this sort of question, so skilfully I ducked and answered: "I haven't played against him this season so I don't really know."

Reporter: "I suppose you have as much chance as the next bloke?"

Me: "Yes, I suppose so."

The evasive action was all in vain. Next day it appeared on the front page in such a way that one could only think the greatest favour Goddard could do Graveney would be to put Ramadhin on to bowl.

This type of statement is no easy one to have to bear when going out to bat before 30,000 people in your First Test after being dropped from the selector's reckoning. Even worse was to follow because I was out for a 'duck'. The only saving factor was that I was dismissed by Gilchrist before Ramadhin could get at me. I should have looked an even larger-mouthed young man had I been put out by the little spinner.

That stormy tour of the West Indies in 1953–54 was made no easier by the attention it attracted in the Press. Certain members of the English Press were hopelessly biased towards the West Indies, whether out of a sense of good manners towards their hosts I have no idea, but whatever the cause we

Englishmen were far from happy at seeing our activities pictured in such a lop-sided fashion in our own newspapers. A feeling was created among the players there that will take a long time dying down.

Some representatives of the more colourful newspapers centred their interest round the 'terrible twins', Trueman and Lock. Their boiling aggression on the field makes them both controversial characters, particularly in an atmosphere from which a sense of balance is rapidly departing. Both of them, with actions no more deplorable than those they produce in England, and with appeals no more vehement than those of well-rehearsed Australians, brought down upon their heads the wrath of the crowds. And out of this glorious welter of temperament and misunderstanding, Lock and Trueman emerged as an immature pair of wicked uncles.

Neither was as black as he was painted and to this day Trueman cannot recall saying some of the words that were attributed to him in various newspapers. Lock and Trueman suffered because their personalities are different from those of the average English cricketer. On a turbulent tour they refused to be placid and so they paid the penalty with much unpleasant and unnecessary publicity.

But just as it is easy enough to criticise cricketers, so it is equally easy to criticise newspapermen, particularly those working for the more popular papers. I would emphasise that on the whole they are a pretty good bunch to get on with.

I only wish they would not be so lavish with their praise of young players. Everybody likes to say they were the first to spot a winner but some of the extravagant forecasts broadsided at the heads of young men playing in their first season is nothing less than harmful. Some day somebody must bring out a supplement to Wisden recording the names and whereabouts of all players of whom it was said in their early days—"this boy will play for England." A good percentage of them will be moderate county players, a great many struggling in the second elevens, and many more struggling to get into their local club side.

Sometimes I think that we experienced players who play most of our cricket away from the main grounds are a little slower to get Test recognition than those belonging to the bigger counties. Down at Cheltenham and Taunton the spotlight is not on us as it is on the men who play at the Oval and Lord's.

And just when I am thinking it is a shame, I remember that by this same argument we generally are allowed to mature as cricketers in our own good time. Nothing spectacular is expected of us and because of that we enjoy our cricket more.

The whole game would have benefited if the Truemans and the Barringtons had been allowed the same privilege. For the sake of this argument geniuses can be discounted. They will make their mark from the age of five upwards no matter what the world may say about them. But geniuses in cricket are far rarer than one would believe.

Probably journalists consider that their privileged class consists of men who report cricket for the 'quality' papers, the men who do not have to ferret out these so-called human, and often inhuman, stories. Yet even they are not beyond criticism. They are allowed to air in their reports their technical knowledge and experience of the game, yet it is a strange feeling next morning to read that you were bowled by a leg-break when the off-break that beat you turned inches. It happened to me facing Ramadhin at the Oval.

The relationship between Press and players will always be a difficult one, but if it gets no worse than it is now it is unlikely to cause a great deal of friction.

At least we in England are spared the unpleasantness that marks criticism in Australia. There religion can cause untold feeling between player and critic.

The most spiteful feuds spring up between journalist and player, journalist and selector. They can last a life time, and most of them can be traced back to the name of the church which they visit on Sundays.

I find life hard enough being judged solely on my cricket without my religion and personal life creeping into the issue.

CHAPTER EIGHTEEN

LOOKING AHEAD

THE accent over the past five years has been on brightening cricket. To meet this requirement various rules have been introduced into the game, and sad to say I have missed the point of most of them.

To my way of thinking there has never been anything wrong with cricket. It was a beautiful game when I played it as a boy, and it has lost none of its beauty with the passing of the years. It is a game that transcends human weakness and error, and it will be a factor in the life of the world long after the men who bowled leg-theory have been forgotten.

I have no love for these tactics that take the spectacle out of the game. Medium paced in-swing bowled to a covey of short-leg fielders is the bane of cricket. It eliminates all those beautiful off-side shots that have had poets searching for words for years. In-swing is a mean, miserly, cramping form of attack, yet I can see no virtue in trying to check it by limiting the number of leg-side fielders, as has been done. Such a method hits harder at the off-spinner than anyone else, and he is essentially an attacking bowler, particularly on a wicket that allows spin.

Artificial regulations are hardly likely to curb those whose lives are devoted to leg-theory, and neither will they contribute anything towards the game. It would be far more to the point for somebody from the top layer of the M.C.C. to speak his mind at a meeting of captains and point out that one or two of their number—and the more he named the better—were strangling the game. Anything that is wrong with cricket can almost invariably be traced back to the captain.

If a bowler bowls defensively it is only because his captain allows it. If a batsman bores everyone to tears with unnecessary defence, the remedy again lies in the hands of the captain. It is in his power to suggest that a player should be dropped.

I doubt very much if any of this need for new rules has come about because of the way the West country teams play their cricket. The five-day Test outlook has never intruded on our approach to a three-day game. We in Gloucestershire and Somerset have believed in making reasonable declarations, and because we have approached a match in the belief that it is worth losing it in an effort to win, our declarations have sometimes brought about our defeat.

Whereupon the wise ones, the cautious ones, have decried it as a silly declaration and gone on their own safety-first ways, driving from the grounds a few more people muttering: "Roll on the football season."

Probably the best of the recent moves to bring more adventure into the game was the one regularising the distance of the boundaries to seventy-five yards. Such a ruling is a boon to batsmen (and bowlers because it tempts batsmen into the big hit) on such grounds as the Oval, but I also feel that wherever the size of the ground permits, the boundary should not be allowed to shrink below seventy-five yards. We ran into trouble from a boundary that was too short, against Sussex in 1957 when Don Smith, the left-handed opening batsman, dropped thunderbolts among the trembling members in the pavilion. While they scuttled for shelter Smith belaboured a hundred and sixty runs, most of them from sweeps and hooks. Afterwards I checked the distance of the stumps from the pavilion and found it to be forty-three paces, a ludicrous, schoolboy hit.

I believe the greatest hunger of the public is for stroke play. They want to see the shots that bring them forward in their seats, the strokes they can replay in imagination on their way home.

And the only way these gems can be brought back to the game in profusion is through the preparation of fast wickets. Let the groundsmen of the country get down to the job of preparing fast, true strips and the demands for 'brighter' cricket will cease. This tendency towards creating pitches that take spin almost from the start, can go too far.

Allow the odds against the batsman to pile up too heavily and the game is finished as a spectacle. The public want to see runs well made with bowlers having enough help from the pitch to be able to spirit away the less gifted performers. The fast wicket is the only one which makes this feasible.

Bowlers of the world will deny this theory with all the vigour and invective they can lay tongues to. But the simple task is to ask a member of the public who were the three greatest cricketers he ever saw, and then sit back while he sorts out the batsmen.

Or take the example of when Middlesex were playing Surrey about the time when both Alec Bedser and Denis Compton were at their peak. I should fancy that for every man in the crowd who went to see Bedser bowl, there were ten to see Compton bat. Unjust I know, but I am convinced it is the truth. The public crave runs, and for many of the older spectators there have probably never been innings to compare with those they saw in the twenties and thirties from the bats of Jack Hobbs, Herbert Sutcliffe, Patsy Hendren and Co. They were all great batsmen on any wicket, yet they were fortunate that in normal conditions they did not have to bat on pitches from which the ball buzzed off from about the third hour onwards.

I am not advocating a return to the doped pitches of the pre-war days, but I do think that immediate steps should be taken to ensure that the bias towards the bowlers is halted now before the game deteriorates from being one of skill into one of chance.

Every spinner is entitled to his help from the pitch, but only after everyone else has had an equal chance to exhibit his skill.

Mechanics of the game apart, I believe the future of cricket lies in week-end matches. The six-day a week programme seems out of touch with modern economic requirements, both from a spectator and playing point of view.

Apart from holiday time, how many nowadays can afford the time to watch cricket through the week? It is little use weeping over empty grounds if most of the games are played when the would-be spectators are at work.

Nor are the public the only ones to suffer from this policy. From my experience, ninety-five per cent of the people in the game today play cricket solely because they like it, not because they see it as a profession producing a lucrative living. In fact a great many of them have trouble finding a winter job, and without one it would be impossible for them to eke out a reasonable standard for themselves and their families. Glamour is all right but bread and butter is useful, too.

The answer lies in week-end cricket with games played over Saturday, Sunday and Monday. To my mind such a scheme has everything to commend it and is one that must come into the reckonings of the advisory county cricket committee before many years pass.

To start with it would uncover an almost completely new watching public, but more important it would revolutionise the game at player level.

Professionals who now spend their spare time counting their hard-earned pennies would find it possible to take all the year round jobs (providing they could get one day off a week) with cricket to supplement their earnings. And into the game would come a fresh, life-giving stream of new material, those top-class players who cannot neglect their businesses for six days a week. With the amount of coaching that is done in our public schools and universities this country must be crammed with talent, yet so much of it goes to waste.

Apart from University amateurs, few bring their talent into the first-class game to develop it. Michael Stewart of Surrey and Bob Gale, Middlesex, are the only two public schoolboys I can recall off-hand, who have joined the ranks of the professionals.

Open up that rich vein and the game must boom and improve, and heaven knows it is good enough now. Yet under the present system the strain on mind and muscle is enormous, and it takes a superhuman effort for a player to maintain a standard of play which satisfies himself. There is no escape from cricket these days. For six days a professional plays for his county and on the seventh he appears in a benefit match.

With a break between matches and a more plentiful supply of players, the jaded feeling would vanish. Bring three or four more counties into the championship and the teams need meet each other only once.

As things stand at present most cricketers rely on their benefits to ensure them of a safe future, and that is a notoriously uneasy way to do it. A run of bad weather can turn a benefit match into financial ruin. No amount of insurance has ever been an adequate substitute for three days of hot weather.

Then all the rest of the vagaries of chance take a hand in a man's benefit. He is a moderate colourless player, essential to his side but unsung, if not unloved, by the followers of the game. Maybe he is injured or out of form during his benefit match, or maybe he is just a run-of-the-mill member of one of the less popular counties, a man who regards a £3,000 benefit as a pretty good effort.

As the benefits of Compton, Hutton, Washbrook and Bedser have soared up over the £10,000 mark there have been suggestions about setting up a benefit pool so that at the end of the season all players receive an equal share of the money.

As a member of a smaller county such a scheme would help me and my colleagues, but I am against it on two counts.

Firstly, once standardisation starts the tax man becomes inquisitive and the Inland Revenue authorities are not people with whom I wish to have any more truck than is absolutely necessary. It has been a difficult enough task keeping the cricketer's benefit tax free without inviting trouble.

Secondly, this benefit money is a personal gift from the people of the county to the player.

When the time comes for my benefit I want to feel that whatever I receive is, apart from individual contributions from outside counties, a gift from the people of Gloucestershire. I shall know then that they have weighed me up, remembered that lanky newcomer who made such an appalling start, forgiven me for the catch I dropped off Tom Goddard on the boundary, made allowance for all those disappointments I must have brought them when my Test career was pursuing its switchback course, and then in the end concluded that perhaps the ten years I have been with the county might have been worse.

For me they could not have been better. They were ten happy years crammed with happy cricket. Here's to ten more!

INDEX